nēhiyawēwin
paskwāwi-pīkiskwēwin

Cree
LANGUAGE OF THE PLAINS

LANGUAGE LAB WORKBOOK

New Edition

nēhiyawēwin
paskwāwi-pīkiskwēwin

Cree
LANGUAGE OF THE PLAINS

LANGUAGE LAB WORKBOOK

Jean L. Okimāsis

 **University of Regina Press**

For questions regarding this license and publication, please contact uofrpress@uregina.ca. To learn more about University of Regina Press's Open Textbook Publishing Program, visit www.uofrpress.ca.

COVER IMAGE: "Powwow at the Battlefords" is © Allen Sapp. All rights reserved. This image is used with the permission of the Estate of Allen Sapp and is not covered by the Creative Commons license used in this book.

COVER AND TEXT DESIGN: John van der Woude, JVDW Designs

Printed and bound in Canada at Imprimerie Gauvin.

Library and Archives Canada Cataloguing in Publication

TITLE: Nēhiyawēwin : paskwāwi-pīkiskwēwin = Cree : language of the Plains. Language lab workbook / Jean L. Okimāsis.

OTHER TITLES: Cree, language of the Plains. Workbook | Cree : language of the Plains. Language lab workbook | Nēhiyawēwin : paskwāwi-pīkiskwēwin. Language lab workbook

NAMES: Okimāsis, Jean L., 1938- author.

DESCRIPTION: New edition. | Includes text in English and Plains Cree.

IDENTIFIERS: Canadiana 20220272123 | ISBN 9780889778856 (softcover)

SUBJECTS: LCSH: Cree language—Problems, exercises, etc. | LCSH: Cree language—Textbooks for foreign speakers—English. | CSH: Cree language—Textbooks for second language learners—English speakers.

CLASSIFICATION: LCC PM987 .O35 2021 Suppl. | DDC 497/.32380071—dc23

University of Regina Press, University of Regina
Regina, Saskatchewan, Canada, S4S 0A2
tel: (306) 585-4758 fax: (306) 585-4699
web: www.uofrpress.ca

U OF R PRESS

Funding for University of Regina Press's Open Textbook Publishing Program and all publications in this program was generously provided by the Government of Saskatchewan.

Contents

Cree 101

Publisher's Note to the 2022 Print Edition

Since the 2018 open access release of Jean Okimāsis's newly revised *Cree: Language of the Plains,* the University of Regina Press—which first published the 1999 and 2004 editions of Dr. Okimāsis's seminal textbook (under its former imprint of the Canadian Plains Research Centre)—has continually had requests for the print version of this updated 2018 edition. With the generous agreement of the author and the University of Regina Open Educational Resources Publishing Program, it gives us much pleasure to bring out this 2022 Language Lab Workbook to accompany the 2021 print edition of the textbook.

Thanks to the generous funding of the Government of Saskatchewan and University of Regina's Open Educational Resources Publishing Program, you can continue to download and share this book and accompanying audio files free of charge with others in either digital or print form by visiting https://www.uregina.ca/oer-publishing/index.html, as long as you provide attribution to Jean L. Okimāsis as the author of the text, and do not change the book or the text in any way, or use it, in part or in whole, for commercial purposes.

To learn more about University of Regina's Open Educational Resources Publishing Program and its mandate to provide students and instructors with easily accessible, peer-reviewed resources, go to https://www.uregina.ca/oer-publishing/open-textbook-program.html.

oskana, Treaty 4 Lands
Regina, Saskatchewan
August 2022

Foreword

This language lab workbook and corresponding recordings have been designed to complement and supplement the Open Access textbook *Cree: Language of the Plains*, which has been redesigned and updated as an introductory study of the grammatical structure of Cree. The language lab sessions attempt to build on that information by presenting drills, exercises, and dialogues to reinforce topics in the textbook. These exercises are not meant to be used entirely on their own to teach Cree but this workbook may serve as a starting point and can be used along with other worksheets and activities.

The Cree language is rich in verb forms, which require agreement with all other grammatical features within a sentence. Note that in both the textbook and the language lab material, nouns, pronouns, and verbs are presented as **animate** or **inanimate**, while verbs are also classified as **transitive** or **intransitive** (depending on the number of nouns or pronouns referred to). Grammatical agreement between verbs, nouns, and pronouns is required.

The precise nature of the Cree language also dictates that many verbs, nouns, and particles must be introduced in the language lab material. The language lab sessions and workbook and the textbook complement each other through vocabulary and the grammatical rules that dictate the use of the right particles.

In the textbook, Appendices B and C contain noun and particle vocabulary lists while Appendices D and E contain verbs. Ultimately these appendices provide students with diverse vocabulary from which to choose when composing Cree sentences. Both the textbook and the workbook aim to teach the same information about the structure of the Cree language. Those studying Cree will experience the precise nature of this language in all its forms: nouns, pronouns, and verbs in their conjugated forms.

The standard roman orthography (SRO) is used throughout this book. As a student of Cree, and probably because I am a speaker of the language, I was amazed that only ten consonants and seven distinct vowels are required to elegantly spell Cree vocabulary. The short vowel sounds of spoken Cree are represented by **a**, **i**, and **o**, while **ā**, **ī**, **ō**, and **ē** represent long vowel sounds. There are also ten consonants: **c**, **h**, **k**, **m**, **n**, **p**, **s**, **t**, **w**, and **y**. I immediately realized that the SRO indeed represented the sounds and the syllables of my language. The wide range of vocabulary, especially the verbs, and the rich grammar were endless but precise. This was the beginning of my journey towards a work that respectfully presents the beautifully constructed Cree language, *nēhiyawēwin*.

Jean L. Okimāsis

Introduction

This language lab workbook has been organized to complement and support the grammatical material presented in the accompanying *Cree: Language of the Plains* textbook. Each lab session, drill, and exercise in this book is accompanied by a cross-reference to the open textbook where you can find a detailed explanation of the specific Cree structure being demonstrated.

Language lab sessions are presented in order of increasing difficulty and each new session builds on the previous ones. Therefore, you are encouraged to undertake the sessions in the order they are presented.

Structure and Features
The language lab sessions have been divided into two sections: Cree 100 and 101. This essentially follows the two halves of the introductory Cree course taught at First Nations University of Canada and elsewhere. Common features in each lab session include drills, dialogue, additional vocabulary, spelling, and the occasional written exercise.

How to Use the Audio Component
In order to best use this language lab workbook, follow the instructions given for each drill or exercise. General instructions related to the audio component are outlined as follows.

Specific instructions for the exercises and dialogues are also given in the language lab sessions.

1. Listen very carefully to each word.
2. Repeat what you hear. The narrator will say each word or sentence twice, then there will be a pause. This will give you time to repeat the Cree word or sentence.
3. In later lab sessions pay particular attention to the pronunciation of each syllable *then* to the contractions of those words in the full sentence of the spoken Cree.
4. If at any time you need to hear the words again, replay the recording, and try again.
5. You will be expected to know all of the vocabulary words used in the spelling and translation exercises.

Verb Conjugation Chart

The following verb conjugation chart is important to keep in mind for many of the lab sessions and will assist you in understanding person-markers. It is important to know what the numbers (1s, 2s, 3s, 3's, 1p, 21, 2p, 3p, and 3'p) stand for because every verb (VAI, VTI, and VTA) follows this numbering system.

1s   indicates   the first person singular (I, me)
2s   indicates   the second person singular (you)
3s   indicates   the third person singular (he, she, it)
3's indicates   the obviative singular (*e.g.:* his/her friend/s)
1p   indicates   the first person plural (we, exclusive)
21   indicates   the first person plural (we, inclusive)
2p   indicates   the second person plural (you)
3p   indicates   the third person plural (they)
3'p indicates   the obviative plural (*e.g.:* their friend/s)

CREE 100

Language Lab Session 1
Sounds and Pronunciation, Minimal Pairs, and Possession

Drill 1.1. Vowel Sounds

Instructions: Pay attention to the vowel sounds as you repeat the following words after me. I will say each word twice. I will begin with the short vowels.

Short vowels: a, i, o

a	ap**i**sīs	a little
	m**ā**m**a**skāc!	amazing!*
	k**i**y**a**	you/your
i	**i**skotēw	a fire
	tān**i**s**i**	how*
	cīk**i**	near
o	**o**kimāhkān	a chief
	ēk**o**si	that's enough*
	nēw**o**	four

Now listen as I say the long vowel sounds twice and repeat after me.

For Drills 1.1 and 1.2, refer to Chapter 2 of the textbook for a detailed overview of the Cree alphabet, short and long vowel sounds, and pronunciation.

An asterisk denotes that the word has other meanings depending on the context.

Long vowels: ā, ī, ō, ē

ā	ācimowin	a story
	māka	but
	nōhtāwiy	my father
ī	nīpin.	It is summer.
	sīsīp	a duck
	sīpiy	a river
ō	ōhow	an owl
	ōcēw	a fly
	sōniyāw	money
ē	ēwako	that's the one
	mēkwāc	presently*
	tēpwē	yell/shout

Drill 1.2. Consonant Sounds

Instructions: Pay attention to the consonant sounds as you repeat the following words after me. I will say each word twice. I will start with the letter "p."

p	**p**īsim	the sun*
	pakān	a nut
	tē**p**akoh**p**	seven
t	**t**awāw.	There is room/space.*
	tohtōsāpoy	milk
	tānitah**t**o?	How many?
k	**k**ohkōs	a pig
	kīspin	if
	si**k**āk	a skunk
c	**c**ēskwa	wait
	cīki	near
	anoh**c**	today*

s	s**ē**māk	right now*
	sisonē	along
	anikwacā**s**(k)	squirrel/gopher
m	**m**īciso	eat
	na**m**ōya	no
	ati**m**	a dog
n	**n**āpēw	a man
	nīso	two
	nimis	my older sister
h	āpi**h**taw	half
	ō**h**i	these (inanimate)
	osī**h**	make it
w	**w**āpos	a rabbit
	nāni**taw**	about/approximately*
	wāhya**w**	far away
y	o**y**ākan	a dish
	yīkowan.	It is foggy.
	ni**y**a	I, me, my

Drill 1.3. Minimal Pairs

Instructions: Listen and repeat the following words after me. I will read the pair of Cree words across each row.

sākahikan	sakahikan
a lake	a nail
niyānan	niyanān
five	us
kisitēw.	kīsitēw.
It is hot.	It is cooked.

Refer to Chapter 3 for more information on minimal pairs: two words that are identical in spelling except for one sound.

Note that each pair of words differs in only one sound (long vowel versus short vowel or different consonants).

nipiy	nīpiy
water	a leaf
asam.	asām
Feed him/her.	a snowshoe
kisisow.	kīsisow.
S/he is hot.	It is cooked.
tāniwā?	tāniwē?
Where is s/he?	Where is it?
ōma	ōta
this	here
pakān	pahkān
a nut	different
mōniyāw	sōniyāw
a Caucasian	money
pōna	kōna
make a fire	snow

Spelling 1.1

Instructions: As I dictate ten Cree words, write them in the spaces provided. I will say each one twice. You can listen to this recording as many times as you like before spelling the word. Check your answers against the key at the back of the book.

1. _____   6. _____

2. _____   7. _____

3. _____   8. _____

4. _____   9. _____

5. _____   10. _____

Drill 1.4. Possessive Body Parts

Instructions: Listen as I narrate each Cree word twice, then repeat after me.

Refer to Chapter 31 for a detailed review of the use of prefixes, which are used to show possession in Independent and Dependent nouns.

mitōn	**a mouth**
nitōn	my mouth
kitōn	your mouth
otōn	his/her mouth
mikot	**a nose**
nikot	my nose
kikot	your nose
okot	his/her nose

miskīsik	**an eye**
niskīsik	my eye
kiskīsik	your eye
oskīsik	his/her eye
mihtawakay	**an ear**
nihtawakay	my ear
kihtawakay	your ear
ohtawakay	his/her ear
miskāt	**a leg**
niskāt	my leg
kiskāt	your leg
oskāt	his/her leg
mispiton	**an arm**
nispiton	my arm
kispiton	your arm
ospiton	his/her arm
micihciy	**a hand**
nicihciy	my hand
kicihciy	your hand
ocihciy	his/her hand
misit	**a foot**
nisit	my foot
kisit	your foot
osit	his/her foot

Language Lab Session 2
Nouns, Imperatives, Numbers, and Greetings

Drill 2.1. Nouns

Instructions: Listen as I narrate the following words twice, then repeat each word. Pay attention to the long and short vowels. I will read the Cree nouns in the left-hand column first, then go down the right-hand column of Cree.

Refer to Chapter 4 for a discussion on animate and inanimate nouns.

sīpiy	a river	pakān	a nut
kinosēw	a fish	nāpēw	a man
piyēsīs	a bird	oyākan	a dish
astotin	a cap/hat	wāpos	a rabbit
akohp	a blanket	iskwēw	a woman
mīciwin	food	tēhtapiwin	a chair
ospwākan	a pipe	mīcisowināhtik	a table
atim	a dog	nihtiy	tea
maskisin	a shoe	minōs	a cat
ayīkis	a frog	kohkōs	a pig
ōtēnaw	a town	sīwinos	a candy

Drill 2.2. Imperatives Said to One Person

For Drills 2.2 through 2.4, refer to Chapter 10 for a review of the Imperative mode, which is used to give orders, commands, invitations, or requests.

Instructions: Listen to and repeat the following commands given to *one person*.

nipā	sleep
waniskā	get up (from bed)
kākīsimo	pray (in traditional manner)
kistāpitēho	brush your teeth
kāsīhkwē	wash your face
sīkaho	comb your hair
paminawaso	prepare a meal
api	sit down
mīciso	eat
minihkwē	drink
pasikō	stand up
pimohtē	walk
nakī	stop (walking)
pimipahtā	run
kwēskī	turn
pāhpi	laugh
kīsitēpo	cook
itwē	say it
nēhiyawē	speak Cree
masinahikē	write*
ākayāsīmo	speak English
sāmin	touch it (animate)
sāmina	touch it (inanimate)
kāsīcihcē	wash your hands

Drill 2.3. Imperatives Said to More than One Person

Instructions: Listen to and repeat the following commands given to *more than one person*. Listen carefully for the "k" sound at the end of each word, which indicates that you are speaking to more than one person.

nipā**k**	sleep
waniskā**k**	get up (from bed)
kākīsimo**k**	pray (in traditional manner)
kistāpitēho**k**	brush your teeth
kāsīhkwē**k**	wash your face
sīkaho**k**	comb your hair
paminawaso**k**	prepare a meal
api**k**	sit down
mīciso**k**	eat
minihkwē**k**	drink
pasikō**k**	stand up
pimohtē**k**	walk
nakī**k**	stop (walking)
pimipahtā**k**	run
kwēskī**k**	turn
pāhpi**k**	laugh
kīsitēpo**k**	cook
itwē**k**	say it
nēhiyawē**k**	speak Cree
masinahikē**k**	write*
ākayāsīmo**k**	speak English
sāmini**hk**	touch it (animate)
sāmina**mok**	touch it (inanimate)
kāsīcihcē**k**	wash your hands

Drill 2.4. Imperatives: Including Yourself

Notice that the "-tān" ending indicates the inclusive: "Let's (you and me, all of us) do something."

Instructions: Listen to and repeat the following words.

nipā**tān**	let's sleep
waniskā**tān**	let's get up (from bed)
kākīsimo**tān**	let's pray (in traditional manner)
kistāpitēho**tān**	let's brush our teeth
kāsihkwē**tān**	let's wash our faces
sīkaho**tān**	let's comb our hair
paminawaso**tān**	let's prepare a meal
api**tān**	let's sit down
mīciso**tān**	let's eat
minihkwē**tān**	let's drink
pasikō**tān**	let's stand up
pimohtē**tān**	let's walk
nakī**tān**	let's stop (walking)
pimipahtā**tān**	let's run
kwēskī**tān**	let's turn
pāhpi**tān**	let's laugh
kīsitēpo**tān**	let's cook
itwē**tān**	let's say it
nēhiyawē**tān**	let's speak Cree
masinahikē**tān**	let's write*
ākayāsīmo**tān**	let's speak English
sāminā**tān**	let's touch it (animate)
sāminē**tān**	let's touch it (inanimate)
kāsīcihcē**tān**	let's wash our hands

Drill 2.5. Numbers 1 to 10

Instructions: Listen and repeat the following terms for numbers. I will read each number twice. I will start with the left-hand column.

For an overview of numbers, refer to Chapter 22.

pēyak	one	nikotwāsik	six
nīso	two	tēpakohp	seven
nisto	three	ayinānēw	eight
nēwo	four	kēkā-mitātaht	nine
niyānan	five	mitātaht	ten

Drill 2.6. Numbers 1 to 10 and Nouns

Instructions: Listen to the following words for counting objects or nouns. I will start reading down the left-hand column and then go down the right one.

pēyak atim	nikotwāsik piyēsīs**ak**
one dog	six birds
nīso minōs**ak**	tēpakohp pahkēkin**wa**
two cats	seven hides
nisto nāpē**wak**	ayinānēw akohp**a**
three men	eight blankets
nēwo ayīkis**ak**	kēkā-mitātaht oyākan**a**
four frogs	nine dishes
niyānan wāpos**wak**	mitātaht masinahikan**a**
five rabbits	ten books

Most nouns are marked in the plural form (as highlighted in bold font).

continued...

pēyak ayīkis	nikotwāsik pakān**ak**
one frog	six nuts
nīso atimw**ak**	tēpakohp wāw**a**
two dogs	seven eggs
nisto iskwēwa**k**	ayinānēw astotin**a**
three women	eight hats/caps
nēwo maskw**ak**	kēkā-mitātaht tēhtapiwin**a**
four bears	nine chairs
niyānan ospwākan**ak**	mitātaht mīcisowināhtik**wa**
five pipes	ten tables

Dialogue 2.1. Greetings

This dialogue drill introduces new information and additional vocabulary not specifically covered in any one section of your textbook.

Instructions: Listen to the following dialogue, which will be repeated twice. Then practise the greetings below with a classmate to supplement your understanding of how to converse with someone you have just met.

A:	tānisi?	Hello, how are you?
B:	namōya nānitaw. kiya māka?	Fine. And you?
A:	pēyakwan. tānisi ē-isiyihkāsoyan?	Just the same. What is your name?
B:	_____ nitisiyihkāson. tānitē ē-ohcīyan?	My name is _____. Where are you from?

A: _____nitohcīn.   I am from _____.
wāhyaw anima ōta ohci,   That's far from here,
māka ōta ēkwa niwīkin.   but I live here now.

tānitē māka kiya ē-ohcīyan? Where are you from?

B: _____niya ohci.   I am from _____.

Dialogue Vocabulary

Instructions: Listen to the following vocabulary and repeat the words after me. I will say each word twice.

tānisi?	How? (colloquially: How are you?)
namōya	no
nānitaw	approximately/about/perhaps
namōya nānitaw	fine (a colloquial expression)
kiya	you (sg.)
māka	but
kiya māka?	And you? (a colloquial expression)
pēyakwan	the same
ē-isiyihkāsoyan	as you are called/named
nitisiyihkāson	I am called/named
tānitē?	Where?
ē-ohcīyan	as you are from _____
nitohcīn	I am from _____
wāhyaw	far away
anima	that
ōta	here
ohcī	be from somewhere
ēkwa	and/now
niwīkin	I live/reside
niya	I/me

Spelling 2.1

Instructions: As I dictate vocabulary from the previous pages, write the words in the spaces provided. You may replay the recording to listen to the words before spelling them. I will dictate each word twice. Check your answers against the key at the back of the book.

1. _____

2. _____

3. _____

4. _____

5. _____

6. _____

7. _____

8. _____

9. _____

10. _____

11. _____

12. _____

13. _____

14. _____

15. _____

16. _____

17. _____

18. _____

19. _____

20. _____

Language Lab Session 3

Greetings, Nouns (Singular, Plural, and Diminutives), and Numbers

Dialogue 3.1. Greetings—Introducing Someone

Instructions: Listen to the following dialogue, which will be repeated twice, then practise the greetings below with a classmate to supplement your understanding of how to converse with someone you have met.

Use the additional vocabulary to enhance your ability to have a basic conversation in Cree.

A: tānisi?   Hello, how are you?

B: ay, takahki!   Great! / Really good!
   kiya māka?   How about you?

A: ēyiwēhk.   I'm getting by.
   awīna wiya awa? [pointing to C]   Who is this?

B: nitōtēm awa.   This is my friend.

     _____isiyihkāsow.   His/her name is _____.

     _____ē-ohcīt.   He/she comes from _____.

A: wāhyaw anima.   That's far away.

    tānisi? [said to C]   How are you?

Dialogue Vocabulary

Instructions: Listen to the following vocabulary and repeat the words. I will say each word twice.

tānisi	How? (colloquially: How are you?)
ay!	colloquial expression meaning "hey!" (with a positive intonation)
takahki	extremely good
kiya	you (sg.)
māka	but
ēyiwēhk	alright/just fine
awīna?	Who?
wiya	him/her
awa	this one (here)
nitōtēm	my friend
isiyihkāsow	He/she is called/named _____.
ē-ohcīt	as he/she comes from _____
wāhyaw	far (away)
anima	that*

Drill 3.1. Nouns—Plurals

Instructions: Listen carefully to the difference in stress patterns of the following nouns as I narrate them in the singular and plural forms. Try to mimic this pronunciation. I will move across the rows saying the singular form first followed by the plural form. Repeat after me.

Refer to Chapter 4 for more information on how to pluralize animate and inanimate nouns using suffixes.

Inanimate Nouns

Singular	*Plural*
wāpikwaniy	wāpikwaniy**a**
maṣinahikan	maṣinahikan**a**
tēhtapiwin	tēhtapiwin**a**
iskwāhtēm	iskwāhtēm**a**

Animate Nouns

I'll read the singular and then the plural forms just as I did before. Repeat after me.

Singular	*Plural*
astis	astis**ak**
atim	atim**wak**
minōs	minōs**ak**
sēhkēpayīs	sēhkēpayīs**ak**
piyēsīs	piyēsīs**ak**
iskwēw	iskwēw**ak**
askihk	askihk**wak**

Spelling 3.1

Instructions: Listen carefully to the words as I say them and spell the words in the spaces provided. I will say each word twice. You can replay the audio several times before attempting to spell the words. Check your answers against the key at the back of the book.

1. _____   8. _____

2. _____   9. _____

3. _____   10. _____

4. _____   11. _____

5. _____   12. _____

6. _____   13. _____

7. _____   14. _____

Drill 3.2. Nouns—Diminutives: Gender and Number

Refer to Chapter 5 for more information on how to create nouns for items or objects that are smaller than the norm.

Instructions: Listen to and repeat the following Cree words. I will say the singular form first followed by the plural form.

asiniy	a rock/stone
asiniy**ak**	rocks/stones
asinīsis	a little rock/pebble
asinīsis**ak**	little rocks/pebbles

sīsīp	a duck
sīsīp**ak**	ducks
sīsīp**isis**	a duckling
sīsīpisis**ak**	ducklings
maskwa	a bear
maskwa**k**	bears
mask**osis**	a cub
maskosis**ak**	cubs
ayīkis	a frog
ayīkis**ak**	frogs
ayīkis**is**	a little frog
ayīkisis**ak**	little frogs
kinēpik	a snake
kinēpik**wak**	snakes
kinēpik**os**	a little snake
kinēpikos**ak**	little snakes
atim	a dog
atim**wak**	dogs
acim**osis**	a little dog/puppy
acimosis**ak**	little dogs/puppies
astotin	a cap/hat
astotin**a**	caps/hats

as**co**cin**is**	a little cap/hat
ascocinis**a**	little caps/hats
tēhtapiwin	a chair*
tēhtapiwin**a**	chairs
cēhcapiwin**is**	a little chair
cēhcapiwinis**a**	little chairs

Drill 3.3. Numbers 11 to 20

For more information on numbers, please see Chapter 22.

Instructions: Listen to the following number terms. I will read each word twice. Repeat after me.

pēyakosāp	eleven
nīsosāp	twelve
nistosāp	thirteen
nēwosāp	fourteen
niyānanosāp	fifteen
nikotwāsosāp	sixteen
tēpakohposāp	seventeen
ayinānēwosāp	eighteen
kēkā-mitātahtosāp	nineteen
nīsitanaw	twenty

Drill 3.4. Conversion Drill

Instructions: For this drill, I will read out a list of nouns, such as *"pēyak atim,"* which means "one dog," followed by a number other than one. Change the singular noun to its plural form. Check your answers against the key at the back of the book.

Before we begin, listen and follow along as I say the following three examples:

Notice that numbers 11 to 19 are represented by numbers 1 to 9 and all have the same additional ending.

pēyak atim	pēyakosāp atim**wak**
nīsosāp	nīsosāp atim**wak**
pēyak minōs	pēyakosāp minōs**ak**

I will now begin the drill. Listen as I read the following nine noun and number combinations, then write the plural form of the noun in the space provided.

Drill Leader	*Student*
1. pēyak sīsīp	nīsosāp _____
2. pēyak maskwa	nistosāp _____
3. pēyak sēhkēpayīs	nēwosāp _____
4. pēyak tēhtapiwin	niyānanosāp _____
5. pēyak wāpikwaniy	nikotwāsosāp _____
6. pēyak askihk	tēpakohposāp _____
7. pēyak ospwākan	ayinānēwosāp _____
8. pēyak kinēpik	kēkā-mitātahtosāp _____
9. pēyak iskwēw	nīsitanaw _____

Spelling 3.2

Instructions: Listen carefully to the words as I say them and spell the words in the spaces provided. I will repeat them twice. You can replay the audio several times before attempting to spell the words. Check your answers against the key at the back of the book.

1. _____   11. _____

2. _____   12. _____

3. _____   13. _____

4. _____   14. _____

5. _____   15. _____

6. _____   16. _____

7. _____   17. _____

8. _____   18. _____

9. _____   19. _____

10. _____   20. _____

Exercise 3.1. Fill in the Blank

Instructions: In this exercise, I will say the Cree word for each of the English translations listed. To help you enhance your listening skills, I will say the words in random order. Listen to and replay the recording as often as necessary. Then write each word on the appropriate line provided. Check your answers against the key at the back of the book.

1. _____
   a pail

2. _____
   a cup

3. _____
   today

4. _____
   a dish

5. _____
   a bear

6. _____
   one

7. _____
   a book

8. _____
   a chair

Negative Imperatives, Diminutives, Verbs, Locatives, and Prepositions

Drill 4.1. Verbs: Negative Imperatives or Commands

Refer to Chapter 13 for an in-depth review of negative imperatives—how to tell someone not to do something.

Instructions: I will say the following negative commands twice in the second person singular (2s), second person plural (2p), and first person plural (21) forms. Listen to the commands said in Cree and then repeat them.

Also note the different form of the negations for first person plural (21) forms.

2s	ēkāwiya pasikō.	Don't stand up. (you, sg.)
2p	ēkāwiya pasikōk.	Don't stand up. (you, pl.)
21	ēkā pasikōtan.	Let's not stand up.
2s	ēkāwiya api.	Don't sit. (you, sg.)
2p	ēkāwiya apik.	Don't sit. (you, pl.)
21	ēkā apitān.	Let's not sit.
2s	ēkāwiya mīciso.	Don't eat. (you, sg.)
2p	ēkāwiya mīcisok.	Don't eat. (you, pl.)
21	ēkā mīcisotān.	Let's not eat.

2s	ēkāwiya ayamihcikē.	Don't read. (you, sg.)
2p	ēkāwiya ayamihcikē**k**.	Don't read. (you, pl.)
21	ēkā ayamihcikē**tān**.	Let's not read.

2s	ēkāwiya kwēskī.	Don't turn. (you, sg.)
2p	ēkāwiya kwēskī**k**.	Don't turn. (you, pl.)
21	ēkā kwēskī**tān**.	Let's not turn.

2s	ēkāwiya itwē.	Don't say it. (you, sg.)
2p	ēkāwiya itwē**k**.	Don't say it. (you, pl.)
21	ēkā itwē**tān**.	Let's not say it.

2s	ēkāwiya nēhiyawē.	Don't speak Cree. (you, sg.)
2p	ēkāwiya nēhiyawē**k**.	Don't speak Cree. (you, pl.)
21	ēkā nēhiyawē**tān**.	Let's not speak Cree.

Drill 4.2. Review of Diminutives

Instructions: Listen to and repeat the following words. I will start narrating the singular nouns on the left then I will say the diminutive form of each noun. Notice that the diminutive forms all end in "*-is*" and are highlighted in bold font only to show the changes to the nouns. Note that some of the nouns change "t" to "c" then add the "*-is*" ending.

The second part of this drill lists the nouns in their plural diminutive forms.

Refer to Chapter 5 in the textbook for more information on this subject.

"-is" changes the noun to a smaller version. For instance, the term "asikan – a stocking/ sock" becomes "asikanis – a little stocking/sock."

Singular Diminutives

minōs	minōs**is**
asikan	asikan**is**
oyākan	oyākan**is**
sīsīp	sīsīpis**is**
astotin	as**co**cin**is**
masinahikan	masinahikan**is**

wāpos	wāpos**is**
maskwa	maskos**is**
ayīkis	ayīkis**is**
tēhtapiwin	cēhcapiwin**is**

Plural Diminutives

I will now read the plural diminutives, starting with the left-hand column. You will notice that one adds the plural form "*-ak*" or "*-a*" after the diminutive ending "*-is.*"

minōsis	minōsis**ak**
asikanis	asikanis**ak**
oyākanis	oyākanis**a**
sīsīpisis	sīsīpisis**ak**
ascocinis	ascocinis**a**
masinahikanis	masinahikanis**a**
wāposis	wāposis**ak**
maskosis	maskosis**ak**
ayīkisis	ayīkisis**ak**
cēhcapiwinis	cēhcapiwinis**a**

Drill 4.3. Review of Verbs

Instructions: Listen to the audio and repeat the following imperative verb forms. I will say the verbs in Cree from left to right on each row.

Refer to Chapters 10 and 11 for more information on verbs in the Imperative mode.

api	mīciso	nipā
sit	eat	sleep
sīkaho	sāmina	pāhpi
comb your hair	touch it	laugh
pimipahtā	nakī	ākayāsīmo
run	stop	speak English
minihkwē	itwē	nēhiyawē
drink	say it	speak Cree
ayamihcikē	masinahikē	kāsīhkwē
read	write	wash your face
kāsīcihcē	waniskā	pimohtē
wash your hands	get up	walk

Drill 4.4. Locatives

For the following three drills, refer to Chapter 9 for more information on how to indicate the location of something or someone.

You will notice the change in meaning just by adding locative suffixes.

Instructions: Listen to and repeat the following words used to show location. Again, I will say the words across each row, starting with the regular noun, followed by the locative form.

1. tēhtapiwin
   a chair
   tēhtapiwin**ihk**
   on the chair

2. wāskahikan
   a house
   wāskāhikan**ihk**
   in/at the house

3. akocikan
   a cupboard*
   akocikan**ihk**
   in the cupboard*

4. oyākan
   a dish/plate
   oyākan**ihk**
   in/on the dish/plate

5. minihkwācikan
   a cup
   minihkwācikan**ihk**
   in the cup

6. tahkascikan
   a refrigerator
   tahkascikan**ihk**
   in/on the refrigerator

7. askihk
   a pail
   askihk**ohk**
   in the pail

8. atāwēwikamik
   a store
   atāwēwikamik**ohk**
   at/in the store

9. mētawēwikamik
   a gymnasium
   mētawēwikamik**ohk**
   in/at the gymnasium

10. mīcisowikamik   mīcisowikamik**ohk**
    a cafe   at/in the cafe

11. mīcisowināhtik   mīcisowināhtik**ohk**
    a table   on the table

12. ōtēnaw   ōtēn**ahk**
    a town   in town

13. nēhiyaw   nēhiyā**nāhk**
    a Cree person   Cree reserve/country

14. pwāta   pwāt**ināhk**
    a Dakota Sioux person   Dakota Sioux reserve/country

15. asinīwipwāt   asinīwipwāt**ināhk**
    an Assiniboine person   Assiniboine reserve/country

16. nahkawiyiniw   nahkawiyin**īnāhk**
    a Saulteaux person   Saulteaux reserve/country

Drill 4.5. Prepositions

Note that the
English translation
doesn't show that
an action has
occurred. Notice
also that most of
the words end in
"-ihk" while four
other words are
altogether different.

Instructions: Listen to the audio and repeat each term after me. I will say each word twice.

nohcimihk	inland (Literally: at the far end or extreme); *e.g.*: (sit) at the far end
asicāyihk	beside/against
ispimihk	up/upstairs
nīhcāyihk	down/downstairs
mohcihk	down (as on the floor/ground)
pīhcāyihk	inside
wayawītimihk	outside
atāmihk	beneath/under the pile
atāmipīhk	underwater
sīpā/sīpāyihk	under (as under the chair)
capasīs	lower down
tahkohc	on top of
sisonē	along (as along the road)
cīki	near
tāwāyihk	in the middle
tastawāyihk	in between
āyētawāyihk/ayitawāyihk	on either side
āstamāstihk	in bright sunlight
ākawāstēhk	in the shade
mohcihtakāhk/mohcihk	on the floor

Drill 4.6. Locatives, Prepositions, and Other Vocabulary

Instructions: Listen as I say the following ten sentences and concentrate on the pronunciation of the locative endings. I will narrate each sentence twice, then repeat after me.

1. oyākan astēw tahkohc tahkascikanihk.
   The dish is on top of the refrigerator.

2. sīpā tēhtapiwinihk mēkwāc nipāw ana minōs.
   That cat is sleeping under the chair right now.

3. ispimihk ici wiyawāw ta-nipāwak.
   They will sleep upstairs.

4. kiyānaw ōta nīhcāyihk kika-nipānaw.
   We (incl.) will sleep down here. (downstairs)

5. mohcihk ōta astā pitamā anihi masinahikana.
   Put those books here on the floor for now.

6. mahti capasīs nawac masinahikē.
   Please write a little lower.

7. cīki atāwēwikamikohk mahti kakwē-nakīhkan.
   Try to park/stop near/close to the store.

8. nētē nohcimihk kiyawāw apik.
   Sit over there at the other end.

9. wayawītimihk aspin awāsisak ē-mētawēcik.
   The children were playing outside.

10. ispimihk anita wiya kī-iskwāhtawīw.
    S/he climbed up there.

Spelling 4.1

Instructions: Listen carefully to the words as I say them, then fill in the missing vowels. I will repeat them twice. You can replay the audio several times before attempting to fill in the missing vowels. Check your answers against the key at the back of the book.

1. ___t___m

2. t___hk___hc

3. s___p___

4. w___y___w___t___m___hk

5. ___sp___m___hk

6. s___s___p

7. t___pw___

8. c___p___s___s

9. ___n___hc

Language Lab Session 5
Greetings, Interrogatives, and Demonstrative Pronouns

Dialogue 5.1. Studying Cree

Instructions: Listen to the following dialogue. The dialogue will be narrated twice, then practise the greetings below with a classmate to supplement your understanding of how to converse with someone who is also studying Cree.

A: tānisi?

B: mōy nānitaw.
awīna kiya?

A: _____ niya nitisiyihkāson.
kiya māka?

B: _____ nitisiyihkāson niya.
ē-kakwē-nēhiyawēyān ōma.

A: nīsta mīna, māka mētoni āyiman.

B: ahpō ētikwē apisīs wīpac ka-nēhiyawānānaw.

A: ahpō ētikwē.

Dialogue Vocabulary

Instructions: We will now go over the dialogue vocabulary. Listen as I narrate the following words and phrases twice, then repeat after me.

tānisi?	How? How are you?
mōy nānitaw.	I am fine. (collapsed version of namōya nānitaw)
awīna?	Who?
kiya	you (sg.)
niya	I/me
nitisiyihkāson	I am named/called _____.
kiya māka?	And you?
ē-kakwē-nēhiyawēyān.	I am trying to speak Cree.
ōma	this* (colloquial usage)
nīsta	me too/also
mīna	also
māka	but
āyiman.	It is difficult.
ahpō ētikwē	perhaps/maybe eventually
wīpac	soon/early
apisīs	a little bit
kika-nēhiyawānaw	We (incl.) will speak Cree.

Drill 5.1. Interrogatives

Instructions: Listen as I narrate the following interrogative words in Cree. I will say them twice, then repeat after me. Pay attention to the stress pattern but also realize that the words are being said out of context.

Refer to Chapter 8 for an overview of the use of interrogatives to ask a question and the question indicator "cî."

tāniwā?	Where is s/he? (animate, sg.)
tāniwēhkāk?	Where are they? (animate, pl.)
tāniwē?	Where is it? (inanimate, sg.)
tāniwēhā?	Where are they? (inanimate, pl.)
tāna?	Which one? (animate, sg.)
tāniki?	Which ones? (animate, pl.)
tānima?	Which one? (inanimate, sg.)
tānihi?	Which ones? (inanimate, pl.)
awīna?	Who? (animate, sg.)
awīniki?	Who? (animate, pl.)
tānisi?	How? / How are you?
tānēhki?	Why?
tānispīhk?	When?
tānitē?	Where?
tānitahto?	How many? (numbers)
tānitahtwāw?	How many times?
tāniyikohk?	How much? (quantity)
tānimayikohk?	How much? (quantity)
tānitowahk?	What kind?
kīko?	What kind?

Exercise 5.1. Fill in the Blank

Instructions: Fill in the blanks using the list of nouns below. I will say each noun listed, moving from left to right. Repeat the word before writing it in the correct space provided. Check your answers against the key at the back of the book.

The words given in questions 1 to 10 are the interrogatives and the nouns to be written in the blanks complete the question. You need to know the classification of nouns and the rules that dictate gender and number agreement to correctly fill in the answers.

Nouns: astotin, nāpēwak, oyākana, iskwēsisak, maskisin, Bill, piyēsīs, tēhtapiwina, masinahikana, nēhiyawak

1. tāniwēhkāk_____?   6. tāna _____?

2. tāniwē _____?   7. tāniki _____?

3. tāniwā _____?   8. tānima _____?

4. tānihi _____?   9. tāniwēhkāk_____?

5. tāniwēhā _____?   10. tāniwēhā _____?

Now that you have finished filling in the blanks, replay the audio and repeat the phrases. Concentrate on the stress and intonation.

Exercise 5.2. Fill in the Blank

Instructions: Listen as I say the following sentences. Fill in the blanks with the appropriate "*-tān*" word. Check your answers against the key at the back of the book.

1. _____ ohci kiya?
   Where are you from?

2. _____ ōma ōta kā-kī-astāyan?
   Why did you put this here?

3. _____ anima?
   What is that?

Drill 5.2. Demonstrative Pronouns

Instructions: Listen as I narrate the following demonstrative pronouns in the animate singular and plural forms. I will read across the row, saying the animate singular pronoun first then the plural pronoun. Repeat the sentences with me while listening.

Refer to Chapter 8 of your textbook for more information on demonstrative pronouns.

Animate Singular	**Animate Plural**
awa sīsīp	**ōki** asikanak
this duck (here)	these socks (here)
awa minōs	**ōki** mitāsak
this cat (here)	these pants (here)
ana wāpos	**aniki** āmowak
that rabbit (there)	those bees (there)

Notice that the singular nouns require only the animate demonstrative pronoun. The plural nouns have both the plural form of the demonstrative pronoun and a plural suffix. Both of these changes are in bold font.

ana awāsis
that child (there)

aniki atimwak
those dogs (there)

nāha askihk
that pail (over there)

nēki minōsak
those cats (over there)

nāha atim
that dog (over there)

nēki awāsisak
those children (over there)

Now I will say the *in*animate singular then the *in*animate plural demonstrative pronouns and repeat them once. Repeat the sentences with me while listening. Again I will go across the row.

Inanimate Singular

Inanimate Plural

ōma masinahikan
this book (here)

ōhi oyākana
these dishes (here)

ōma astotin
this hat (here)

ōhi masinahikana
these books (here)

anima oyākan
that dish (there)

anihi tēhtapiwina
those chairs (there)

anima mōhkomān
that knife (there)

anihi mōhkomāna
those knives (there)

nēma tēhtapiwin
that chair (over there)

nēhi maskisina
those shoes (over there)

nēma maskisin
that shoe (over there)

nēhi astotina
those hats (over there)

Exercise 5.3. Demonstrative Pronouns

Instructions: Listen to the following sentences as I narrate them and write the appropriate demonstrative pronouns in the spaces provided. Check your answers against the key at the back of the book.

1. _____atim āsay kī-mīcisow.
   This dog ate already.

2. _____nāpēsisak wī-ayamihcikēwak.
   These boys are going to read.

3. _____awāsisak nōhtē-mīcisowak.
   Those (over there) children want to eat.

4. nikāwiy nitawēyihtam _____oyākan.
   My mother wants **this** dish.

5. kikī-wāpahtēn cī _____astotin kā-kī-atāwēyān?
   Did you see **that** hat that I bought?

6. pētā _____masinahikana ōta.
   Bring **those (over there)** books here.

7. kī-nitawēyihtam ana _____maskisina.
   S/he wanted **those** shoes.

8. āsay cī kī-kisīpēkinamwak _____oyākana?
   Did they already wash **those** dishes?

9. kī-wanihkēwak aniki _____minihkwācikana.
   They forgot **those (over there)** cups.

10. _____minōs na-nipāw mēkwāc.
    That cat is sleeping at the moment/right now.

Spelling. 5.1

Instructions: Listen carefully to the words as I say them and fill in the missing vowels in the words below. I will repeat the words twice. You can replay the audio several times before attempting to fill in the blanks. Check your answers against the key at the back of the book.

1. t__˙_n___hk___
2. k___sp__n
3. n___p__s__s
4. p__y__s__s
5. t___n__t__
6. t__p__k__hp
7. t__n__
8. n__k__
9. t__n__w__hk__k
10. t__n__w__h__

11. ___w___s___s
12. ___skw___s___s
13. ___skw__ht__m
14. t__n__s__
15. m__n__s
16. ___n___hc
17. n__h__
18. t__n__w__
19. ___spw__k__n
20. ___st__t__n__

When you have finished this exercise, replay the audio and repeat the words as they are being said. Make note of the short and long vowel sounds.

Spelling 5.2.

Instructions: Listen carefully to the verbs as I dictate them and fill in the missing vowels. I will repeat the words twice. You can replay the audio several times before attempting to fill in the correct vowel. Check your answers against the key at the back of the book.

1. __p__

2. k__w__

3. n__k__

4. s__k__h__

5. __tw__

6. p__s__k__

7. n__p__

8. kw__sk__

9. m__c__s__

10. m__s__n__h__k__

11. n__p__w__

12. m__n__hkw__

Imperatives and Independent Mode, Affirmative and Negative Statements, Polarity Questions, and Locatives

Drill 6.1. Imperatives and Independent Mode

For the first two drills, refer to Chapters 10 and 11 for more explanations.

Instructions: Listen to the audio and repeat the following verbs. I will narrate the verbs moving across the rows. First, I will say the verb in the Imperative form of the second person singular (2s), second person plural (2p), or first person plural (21) in the left-hand column. Then I will say the verb in this stem form inflected for various forms of the Independent mode in the right-hand column. It may help for you to underline or highlight the verb stem within the inflected form. The first one is done for you.

Imperatives		Independent	
2s	**pāhpi**	1s	ni**pāhpi**n
2s	mīciso	1s	nimīcison
2s	pimohtē	1s	nipimohtān

2s	masinahikē	1s	nimasinahikān
2s	kīwē	2s	kikīwān
2s	mīciso	2s	kimīcison
2s	atoskē	2s	kitatoskān
2s	itohtē	2s	kititohtān
2p	pāhpik	1p	nipāhpinān
2p	mīcisok	1p	nimīcisonān
2p	masinahikēk	1p	nimasinahikānān
2p	nēhiyawēk	1p	ninēhiyawānān
2p	pimohtēk	1p	nipimohtānān
21	mīcisotān	21	kimīcisonaw
21	atoskētān	21	kitatoskānaw
21	pimipahtātān	21	kipimipahtānaw
21	kīwētān	21	kikīwānaw

Drill 6.2. Affirmatives and Negatives in Present Tense

Instructions: Listen to the audio and repeat the following sentences in the *present* tense. I will say the affirmative statement first, followed by the negative form.

Affirmative Statement

Negative Statement

Note that the placement of the term "namōya" changes the sentence to a negative statement.

1. nipāhpin.
   I laugh.

   namōya nipāhpin.
   I do not laugh.

2. nimīcison.
   I eat.

   namōya nimīcison.
   I do not eat.

3. kinipān.
   You (sg.) sleep.

   namōya kinipān.
   You (sg.) are not asleep.

4. kipimohtān.
   You (sg.) walk.

   namōya kipimohtān.
   You (sg.) are not walking.

5. kimasinahikān.   namōya kimasinahikān.
   You (sg.) write.   You (sg.) do not write.

6. nēhiyawēw.   namōya nēhiyawēw.
   S/he speaks Cree.   S/he does not speak Cree.

7. mostohtēw.   namōya mostohtēw.
   S/he goes on foot.   S/he does not go on foot.

Drill 6.3. Affirmatives and Negatives in Past Tense

Again, notice that the placement of the term "namōya" changes the sentence to a negative statement.

Instructions: Listen to the audio and repeat the following sentences in the *past* tense. I will say the affirmative statement first, followed by the negative statement, moving across the row.

Affirmative Statement	Negative Statement
1. nikī-kīwānān.	namōya nikī-kīwānān.
We (excl.) went home.	We (excl.) did not go home.
2. nikī-mīcisonān.	namōya nikī-mīcisonān.
We (excl.) ate.	We (excl.) did not eat.
3. kikī-itohtānaw.	namōya kikī-itohtānaw.
We (incl.) went.	We (incl.) did not go.
4. kikī-pāhpinaw.	namōya kikī-pāhpinaw.
We (incl.) laughed.	We (incl.) did not laugh.
5. kikī-nipānāwāw.	namōya kikī-nipānāwāw.
You (pl.) slept.	You (pl.) did not sleep.
6. kikī-atoskānāwāw.	namōya kikī-atoskānāwāw.
You (pl.) worked.	You (pl.) did not work.

7. kī-pimipahtāwak.   namōya kī-pimipahtāwak.
    They ran.   They did not run.

8. kī-itohtēwak.   namōya kī-itohtēwak.
    They went.   They did not go.

Drill 6.4. Polarity Questions

Instructions: Listen to the audio and repeat the following sentences after me. Keep in mind that you can easily just say "yes" or "no" in response to the questions below.

Refer to Chapter 6 for a review of polarity questions.

1. **Q. kinēhiyawān cī?**   **Do you (sg.) speak Cree?**
    A. āha, ninēhiyawān.   Yes, I speak Cree.
    A. namōya ninēhiyawān;   I do not speak Cree;
       nitākayāsīmon piko.   I speak English only.
    A. namōya, namōya ninēhiyawān. No, I do not speak Cree.

Refer to Chapter 9 for the vocabulary in this drill.

2. **Q. kikī-mīcison cī?**   **Did you (sg.) eat?**
    A. āha nikī-mīcison.   Yes, I ate.
    A. namōya nikī-mīcison;   I did not eat;
       nikī-mwēstasisinin.   I was late.
    A. namōya, namōya nikī-mīcison. No, I did not eat.
    A. namēskwa nikī-mīcison.   I did not eat yet.

3. **Q. kikī-kīwān cī.**   **Did you (sg.) go home?**
    A. āha, nikī-kīwān.   Yes, I went home.
    A. namōya nikī-kīwān;   I did not go home;
       nikī-otami-atoskān.   I was busy working
    A. namōya, namōya nikī-kīwān.   No, I did not go home.

4. **Q. kikī-nipān cī?** **Did you (sg.) sleep?**

A. āha, nikī-nipān. Yes, I slept.

A. namōya nikī-nipān; I did not sleep;
nikī-atoskān. I worked.

A. namōya, namōya nikī-nipān. No, I did not sleep.

5. **Q. kikī-mīcisonāwāw cī?** **Did you (pl.) eat?**

A. āha, nikī-mīcisonān. Yes, we (excl.) ate.

A. namōya nikī-mīcisonān; We (excl.) did not eat;
nikī-kīsitēponān. we cooked.

A. namōya, namōya No, we (excl.) did not eat.
nikī-mīcisonān.

Drill 6.5. Locative Prepositions

Instructions: Listen to the audio and repeat the following words after me. I will dictate the words according to numerical order. These terms are used to point to a specific location.

1. nohcimihk   inland; at the far end
2. nīhcāyihk   below; downstairs
3. atāmihk   beneath; under
4. wayawītimihk   outside; outdoors
5. sīpā   under; underneath something
6. ispimihk   up; high up; upstairs
7. atāmipīhk   underwater
8. pīhcāyihk   in; inside; indoors

Spelling 6.1

Instructions: Listen carefully to the following words as I say them and fill in the missing vowels in the words below. I will repeat the words twice. You can replay the audio several times before filling in the blanks. Check your answers against the key at the back of the book.

1. n__p__hp__n__n
2. n__h__y__w__w
3. k__m__c__s__n
4. k__n__p__n__w__w
5. n__p__w__k
6. k__m__s__n__h__k__n
7. n__m__c__s__n__n
8. m__st__ht__w
9. k__n__h__y__w__n__w
10. k__p__hp__n__w

11. m__s__n__h__k__w
12. m__c__s__w__k
13. n__n__h__y__w__n
14. n__t__t__sk__n__n
15. p__hp__w
16. n__h__y__w__w__k
17. p__m__ht__w__k
18. k__m__c__s__n__w__w
19. n__m__st__ht__n__n
20. __t__sk__w

Spelling 6.2

Instructions: Listen to the following words and sentences as I say them in numerical order and place macrons over the vowels with the long sounds, if there are any. You may listen to the recording several times before placing the macrons. Check your answers against the key at the back of the book.

Note that periods have been placed at the end of sentences.

1. atamihk
2. namoya
3. pahpiw.
4. atoskew.
5. niyanan
6. tepakohp
7. taniwe.
8. anohc
9. napew
10. nikotwasik
11. iskwesis
12. moswa
13. minos
14. niyanan
15. masinahikan
16. nimasinahikan.
17. soniyaw
18. sipiy
19. wahyaw
20. apisis
21. tapwe.

Dialogue 6.1. Lunch Time

Instructions: Listen to the following dialogue, illustrating a conversation between a mother and her son as she calls her children in for lunch. The dialogue will be repeated twice. Then practise the dialogue with a classmate.

Mother:	Darren, tāniwēhkāk awāsisak?
Darren:	wayawītimihk mētawēwak.
Mother:	āstamitik awāsisak, pē-mīcisok ēkwa.
Darren:	kīkwāy?
Mother:	pē-pīhtokwēk sēmāk.
Darren:	ahāw.
	nitawi-mīcisotān!
Mother:	kāsīcihcēk ēkwa.

Dialogue Vocabulary

Instructions: We will now review the dialogue vocabulary. Listen to the following words and phrases, which I will repeat twice. Then repeat the words and phrases after me.

tāniwēhkāk?	Where are they?
awāsisak	children
wayawītimihk	outside/outdoors
mētawēwak.	They are playing outside.
āstamitik.	Come. (said to more than one person)
pē-	preverb denotes that the action comes towards the speaker.
mīcisok.	Eat. (said to more than one person.)
ēkwa	and/now
kīkwāy?	What?
pīhtokwēk	come in/go in (depending where the speaker is)
sēmāk	right away/immediately
ahāw	okay
nitawi-	go and ____ (preverb)
mīcisotān.	Let's eat.
kāsīcihcēk!	Wash your hands! (said to more than one person)

Language Lab Session 7

Preverbs and Inanimate Intransitive Verbs— Weather, Days of the Week, and Seasons

Drill 7.1. Verbs with Preverbs

Refer to Chapter 6 for a detailed explanation of preverbs and their use.

Instructions: Listen to the audio. I will say each sentence twice, then repeat after me. You will notice that the preverbs make a difference to the command.

1.	kīwē!	Go home! (sg.)
2.	**ati**-kīwē ēkwa!	Be on your way home!
3.	**pē**-kīwē sēmāk!	Come home immediately!
4.	mētawē!	Play! (sg.)
5.	**nitawi**-mētawē!	Go and play! (sg.)
6.	**pōni**-mētawēk ēkwa!	Stop playing now! (pl.)
7.	waniskā!	Get up/wake up! (sg.)
8.	**kakwē**-waniskā ēkwa.	Try getting up.
9.	atoskēk!	Work! (pl.)
10.	**kakwē-sōhki**-atoskēk.	Try working hard.
11.	**nitawi-sōhki**-atoskētān.	Let's go and work hard.

12. masinahikēw ana nāpēsis.	That boy writes.
13. **nihtā**-masinahikēw ana nāpēsis.	That boy can write well.
14. **ati-nihtā**-masinahikēw ēkwa ana nāpēsis.	That boy is on his way to being a good writer.
15. **māci-nihtā**-masinahikēw ēkwa wiya.	S/he is starting to write well.
16. mīcisowak mēkwāc awāsisak.	The children are presently eating.
17. **kīsi**-mīcisowak ēkwa awāsisak.	The children are finished eating.
18. mahti **kakwē-kīsi**-mīcisok.	Please try to finish eating. (pl.)
19. **pa-pēyako**-mētawēw māna ana iskwēsis.	That girl usually plays by herself. (alone)
20. **nōhtē**-atoskēwak.	They want to work.
21. **nōhtē-nihtā**-ayamihcikēwak ōki awāsisak.	These children want to be able to read well.
22. **pē**-yōskapi ōta.	Come and sit here. (on a soft seat) (pl.)

Drill 7.2. Inanimate Intransitive Verbs (VII-1)—Weather

Instructions: Listen to the audio and notice that the Independent word translates to a whole sentence in English. I will say the word in each row first in the Independent mode and then in the Conjunct mode. Repeat the words more than once so that you remember the terms for weather.

First, I will ask the question:

Q. tānisi ē-isiwēpahk?   **What is the weather like?**

For the next three drills, refer to Chapter 14 for a detailed explanation of the use of inanimate intransitive verbs to express natural happenings or states such as weather, days of the week, and seasons.

The following are possible answers to this question.

Independent Mode	English Translation	Conjunct Mode
wāsēskwan.	It is sunny.	ē-wāsēskwahk
yōtin.	It is windy.	ē-yōtik
sōhkiyowēw.	It is a strong wind.	ē-sōhkiyowēk
kimiwan.	It is raining.	ē-kimiwahk
kimiwasin.	It is drizzling.	ē-kimiwasik
pahkipēstāw.	Raindrops are beginning to fall.	ē-pahkipēstāk
sīkipēstāw.	It is pouring rain.	ē-sīkipēstāk
kaskanawipēstāw.	It is misty. (light drizzle)	ē-kaskaniwipēstāk
yīkwaskwan.	It is cloudy.	ē-yīkwaskwahk
yīkowan.	It is foggy.	ē-yīkowahk
pīwan.	It is drifting. (snow)	ē-pīwahk
mispon.	It is snowing.	ē-mispok
kisināw.	It is very cold. (weather only)	ē-kisināk
tahkāyāw.	It is cold. (temperature)	ē-tahkāyāk
aywēstin.	It is calm.	ē-aywēstik
papēskwatāstan.	The snow is drifting into piles/ridges.	ē-papēskwatāstahk
kāmwātan.	It is calm.	ē-kāmwātahk
māyi-kīsikāw.	It's a miserable day.	ē-māyi-kīsikāk
maci-kīsikāw.	It's a miserable day.	ē-maci-kīsikāk

Drill 7.3. VII-1—Time of Day

Instructions: Listen to the audio. I will say the word in each row first in the Independent mode and then in the Conjunct mode. Repeat the words more than once so that you remember the terms for the time of day.

Independent Mode	English Translation	Conjunct Mode
kīsikāw.	It is day.	ē-kīsikāk
kīkisēpāyāw.	It is morning.	ē-kīkisēpāyāk
āpihtā-kīsikāw.	It is midday.	ē-āpihtā-kīsikāk
otākosin.	It is evening.	ē-otākosik
tipiskāw.	It is dark/night.	ē-tipiskāk
āpihtā-tipiskāw.	It is midnight.	ē-āpihtā-tipiskāk
wawāninākwan.	It is twilight.	ē-wawāninākwahk

Drill 7.4. VII-1—Days of the Week

Instructions: Listen to the audio. I will say the word in each row first in the Independent mode and then in the Conjunct mode. Repeat the words more than once so that you remember the terms for the days of the week.

Independent Mode	English Translation	Conjunct Mode
pēyako-kīsikāw.	It is the first day. (Monday)	ē-pēyako-kīsikāk
nīso-kīsikāw.	It is the second day. (Tuesday)	ē-nīso-kīsikāk
nisto-kīsikāw.	It is the third day. (Wcdncsday)	ē-nisto-kīsikāk
nēwo-kīsikāw.	It is the fourth day. (Thursday)	ē-nēwo-kīsikāk

niyānano-kīsikāw.   It is the fifth day.   ē-niyānano-kīsikāk
                    (Friday)
nikotwāso-kīsikāw. It is the sixth day.   ē-nikotwāso-kīsikāk
                    (Saturday)
ayamihēwi-kīsikāw. It is prayer day.   ē-ayamihēwi-kīsikāk
                    (Sunday)

Listen as I narrate additional vocabulary to express time. Repeat after me.

wāpahki	tomorrow
awasi-wāpahki	the day after tomorrow
otākosīhk	yesterday
awasotākosīhk	the day before yesterday

Spelling 7.1

Instructions: Listen as I say the following weather terms then place macrons over the appropriate long vowel sounds. I will say each term twice. Check your answers against the key at the back of the book.

1. yotin

2. sikipestaw

3. piwan

4. pahkipestaw

5. ayamihewi-kisikaw

6. kisinaw

7. waseskwan

8. yikwaskwan

9. newo-kisikaw

10. yikowan

11. tahkayaw

12. sohkiyowew

Spelling 7.2

Instructions: Fill in the missing vowels as I dictate the following words. I will repeat them twice. Remember that long vowel sounds require macrons. You can replay the audio several times before attempting to fill in the blanks. Check your answers against the key at the back of the book.

1. k__m__w__n

2. n__s__-k__s__k__w

3. __yw__st__n

4. p__p__skw__t__st__n

5. k__mw__t__n

6. n__st__-k__s__k__w

7. w__s__skw__n

8. s__k__p__st__w

9. p__w__n

10. n__y__n__n__-k__s__k__w

11. m__sp__n

12. k__sk__n__w__p__st__w

13. y__kw__skw__n

14. n__k__tw__s__-k__s__k__w

15. t__hk__y__w

16. k__m__w__s__n

17. __y__m__h__w__-k__s__k__w

18. p__y__k__-k__s__k__w

19. y__t__n

20. y__k__w__n

Drill 7.5. Inanimate Intransitive Verbs with Preverbs

Refer to both Chapters 6 and 14 for this drill.

Instructions: Listen to the audio and repeat the following sentences after me. I will say each sentence twice.

1. māci-mispon. It is beginning to snow.
2. pōni-mispon. It stopped snowing.
3. māci-kimiwan. It is beginning to rain.
4. pōni-kimiwan. It stopped raining.
5. pē-yīkwaskwan. It is getting cloudy.
   (in the distance)

Drill 7.6. Seasons

Refer to Chapter 15 for further information for this drill.

Instructions: Listen to the audio and repeat the following sentences after me. I will say each sentence twice, starting with the *present* tense.

Present Tense

1. pipon. It is winter.
2. sīkwan/miyoskamin. It is spring.
3. nīpin. It is summer.
4. takwākin. It is fall.

Now I will narrate the terms used to refer to seasons *past*. Notice that the ending "*-ohk*" does not work for the term "*miyoskamin*" in the past, unlike the other terms here.

Past

1. piponohk last winter/this past winter
2. sīkwanohk last spring/this past spring
3. nīpinohk last summer/this past summer
4. takwākohk last fall/this past fall

Next, I will dictate the same terms used to refer to *future* seasons.

Future

1. pipohki	when it is winter/this coming winter
2. sīkwahki/miyoskamiki	when it is spring/this coming spring
3. nīpihki	when it is summer/this coming summer
4. takwākiki	when it is fall/this coming fall

Exercise 7.1. Matching: Weather, Days of the Week, and Seasons

Instructions: Match column A with the correct meaning in column B. Listen as I say the words in column A, then place the number beside the correct meaning in column B. Check your answers against the key at the back of the book.

A	**B**
1. mispon.	a. ___ It is windy.
2. nīpin.	b. ___ It is cold. (refers to temperature)
3. nisto-kīsikāw.	c. ___ It is fall/autumn.
4. wāsēskwan.	d. ___ It is snowing.
5. takwākin.	e. ___ It is spring.
6. yōtin.	f. ___ It is summer.
7. kisināw.	g. ___ It is clear/sunny.
8. ayamihēwi-kīsikāw.	h. ___ It is Wednesday/the third day.
9. sīkwan.	i. ___ It is very cold. (refers to weather)
10. tahkāyāw.	j. ___ It is prayer day.

Spelling 7.3

Instructions: Fill in the missing vowels as I dictate the following terms for weather and seasons. I will repeat them twice. Remember that long vowel sounds require macrons. You can replay the audio several times before attempting to fill in the blanks. Check your answers against the key at the back of the book.

1. n__p__n

2. p__p__n

3. s__kw__n

4. p__p__n__hk

5. m__y__sk__m__k__

6. w__s__skw__n

7. t__kw__k__hk

8. k__s__n__w

9. t__kw__k__n

10. n__p__n__hk

11. m__y__sk__m__n

12. p__p__hk__

13. s__kw__n__hk

14. n__p__hk__

Language Lab Session 8

Animate Intransitive Verbs and Pronouns, Months, and Dates

Drill 8.1. Review of Imperatives

Instructions: Listen to the audio and repeat the following commands after me. Note that the placement of the Cree term to tell someone "Don't (do something)" is located before verb forms 2s, 2p, and 21. I will start with the affirmative commands in the Imperative mode and say each word twice.

Refer to Chapter 10 for a review of the Imperative mode, which is used to give orders, commands, invitations, or requests.

Imperative Mode

2s	api!	Sit!
2p	apik!	Sit!
21	apitān.	Let's sit.

Negative Imperative

2s	ēkāwiya api!	Don't sit!
2p	ēkāwiya apik!	Don't sit!
21	ēkāwiya apitān.	Let's not sit.

Drill 8.2. Conjugation of Animate Intransitive Verbs

For a detailed explanation of the conjugation of animate intransitive verbs, refer to Chapter 11.

Instructions: Listen as I say each sentence twice, then repeat after me. You may want to review this drill more than once. I will start with the *present* tense.

Notice that the vowel "o" on the verb stem does not change.

Present Tense

1s	**ni**mīcison.	**I** eat.
2s	**ki**mīcison.	**You** (sg.) eat.
3s	mīcisow.	**S/he** eats.
3's	mīcisoyiwa.	**His/her** _____ (sg.) eats.
1p	**ni**mīciso**nān**.	**We** (excl.) eat.
21	**ki**mīciso**naw**.	**We** (incl.) eat.
2p	**ki**mīciso**nāwāw**.	**You** (pl.) eat.
3p	mīciso**wak**.	**They** eat.
3'p	mīcisoyiwa.	**His/her**____ (pl.) eat.

Now I will narrate the following sentences in the *past* tense. Notice that the past tense form is underlined for emphasis. Repeat after me.

Past Tense

1s	**ni**<u>kī</u>-pahkwēsikanihkā**n**.	I **made** bannock.
2s	**ki**<u>kī</u>-pahkwēsikanihkā**n**.	You (sg.) **made** bannock.
3s	<u>kī</u>-pahkwēsikanihkē**w**.	S/he **made** bannock.
3's	<u>kī</u>-pahkwēsikanihkē**yiwa**.	His/her _____ (sg.) **made** bannock.
1p	**ni**<u>kī</u>-pahkwēsikanihkā**nān**.	We (excl.) **made** bannock.
21	**ki**<u>kī</u>-pahkwēsikanihkā**naw**.	We (incl.) **made** bannock.

2p	**kikī**-pahkwēsikanihkā**nāwāw**.	You (pl.) **made** bannock.
3p	**kī**-pahkwēsikanihkē**wak**.	They **made** bannock.
3'p	**kī**-pahkwēsikanihkē**yiwa**.	His/her _____ (pl.) **made** bannock.

Drill 8.3. Personal Pronouns

Instructions: Listen to the audio and repeat the following pronouns.

1s	niya	I/me
2s	kiya	you (sg.)
3s	wiya	her/him/it
1p	niyanān	we/us (excl.)
21	kiyānaw	we/us (incl.)
2p	kiyawāw	you (pl.)
3p	wiyawāw	they/them

For the next two drills and others below, refer to Chapter 7 for more information on personal pronouns and inclusive pronouns.

Drill 8.4. Inclusive Personal Pronouns

Instructions: Listen as I say the following inclusive pronouns, then repeat after me.

1s	nīsta	me too/also
2s	kīsta	you too/also (sg.)
3s	wīsta	him/her too/also
1p	nīstanān	us too/also (excl.)
21	kīstanaw	us too/also (incl.)
2p	kīstawāw	you too/also (pl.)
3p	wīstawāw	them/they too/also

Recall that these pronouns can mean "me too/also," "you too/also," etc., depending on the situation.

Drill 8.5. More Animate Intransitive Verbs

Instructions: As you listen to the audio and repeat the following verbs, remember that they are in the Imperative mode and say each command twice.

atoskē	work
māto	cry
sēsāwipahtā	jog
pāhpi	laugh
nīmā	pack a lunch
kiyokē	visit
pwātisimo	dance pow-wow
sipwēhtē	leave
pahkwēsikanihkē	make bannock
nīmihito	dance
kotawē	make a fire
itahtopiponē	be of a certain age

Drill 8.6. Imperatives and Personal Pronouns

You can review Chapters 7 and 10 to help with this drill.

Instructions: Listen to the audio and repeat the following words after me. While doing so, remember that the second word is a personal pronoun. I will read each column beginning at the top.

2s	api **kiya**		2s	pimohtē **kiya**
2s	atoskē **kiya**		2s	pāhpi **kiya**
2s	pwātisimo **kiya**		2s	pimipahtā **kiya**
2s	māto **kiya**		2s	nīmihito **kiya**
2p	pasikō**k kiyawāw**		2p	ākayāsīmo**k kiyawāw**
2p	waniskā**k kiyawāw**		2p	nipā**k kiyawāw**
2p	kīwē**k kiyawāw**		2p	mīciso**k kiyawāw**
21	nahapi**tān kiyānaw**		21	nēhiyawē**tān kiyānaw**
21	nīmā**tān kiyānaw**		21	minihkwē**tān kiyānaw**
21	sipwēhtē**tān kiyānaw**		21	sēsāwipahtā**tān kiyānaw**
21	kīsitēpo**tān kiyānaw**		21	kotawē**tān kiyānaw**

Drill 8.7. Inclusive Personal Pronouns and Animate Intransitive Verbs

Instructions: Listen to the audio and repeat the following sentences. Note that the sentences translate as "me too/also," "you too/also," etc.

1s niwī-kawisimon **nīsta**.
I am going to bed too.

2s kiwī-ayamihcikān cī **kīsta**.
Are you (sg.) going to read too?

3s kī-mīcisow āsay **wīsta**.
S/he, too, ate already.

1p **nīstanān** nikī-atoskānān otākosīhk.
We, too, worked yesterday.

21 **kīstanaw** kika-nitawi-sēsāwipahtānaw mwēstas.
We, too, will go and jog later.

2p kikī-mīcisonāwāw cī **kīstawāw**.
Did you (pl.) eat too?

3p wī-pē-kiyokēwak anohc **wīstawāw**.
They, too, are intending to come to visit today.

Drill 8.8. Months

Refer to Chapter 15 for a more detailed explanation of the use of inanimate intransitive verbs to refer to the passage of time.

Instructions: Listen to the audio and repeat the following words. I will say each term twice. Notice that the Cree word for moon, "*pīsim*," is constant in these names for the months.

1.	kisē-pīsim	January
2.	mikisiwi-pīsim	February
3.	niski-pīsim	March
4.	ayīki-pīsim	April
5.	sākipakāwi-pīsim	May
6.	pāskāwihowi-pīsim	June
7.	paskowi-pīsim	July
8.	ohpahowi-pīsim	August
9.	takwāki-pīsim/nōcihitowi-pīsim	September
10.	pimihāwi-pīsim	October
11.	iyīkopīwi-pīsim	November
12.	pawācakinasīsi-pīsim	December

Drill 8.9. Numbers 20 to 31

Refer to Chapter 22 for more information on numbers.

Instructions: Listen to the audio and repeat the following words for numbers. I will say each number twice. Remember that, except for the numbers 20 and 30, one adds the teen numbers to 20.

20	nīsitanaw
21	nīsitanaw pēyakosāp
22	nīsitanaw nīsosāp
23	nīsitanaw nistosāp
24	nīsitanaw nēwosāp
25	nīsitanaw niyānanosāp
26	nīsitanaw nikotwāsosāp
27	nīsitanaw tēpakohposāp

28   nīsitanaw ayinānēwosāp

29   nīsitanaw kēkā-mitātahtosāp

30   nistomitanaw

31   nistomitanaw pēyakosāp

Drill 8.10. Month, Date, and Day of the Week

Instructions: Read along as I narrate the following sentences and note the suffixes "*-yiki*," which is used for future days, and "*-ihci*" and "*-ki*," which are used for calendar dates showing that a person is going to do something.

Refer to Chapter 15 for a detailed explanation of seasons, months, weekdays, and time.

The sentences below are for practice and will help you gain a better understanding of Future Conditional forms.

1.   ayēnānēw akimāw awa takwāki-pīsim.
    This Autumn Moon is counted eight. *or*
    It is September 8th.

2.   nīso-kīsikāw anohc, niyānanosāp akimāw awa
        takwāki-pīsim.
    It is Tuesday, the 15th of September.

3.   nīsosāp akim**ihci** ayīki-pīsim cōniy ta-tipiskam.
    When the Frog Moon is counted twelve, Joan will have
        a birthday. *or*
    Joan will have her birthday on the 12th of April.

4.   nikotwāso-kīsikā**yiki** nōhkom wī-pē-kiyokēw.
    When it is the sixth day, my grandmother is coming to
        visit. *or*
    My grandmother is coming to visit on Saturday.

5.   ayamihēwi-kīsikā**ki** niwī-nipān kapē-kīsik.
    When it is Sunday, I am going to sleep all day.

Language Lab Session 9

Animate Intransitive Verbs (continued), Independent and Conjunct Modes

Drill 9.1. Independent Mode

For a detailed explanation of the conjugation of animate intransitive verbs, refer to Chapter 11.

Remember that the "ē" changes to an "ā" in 1s, 2s, 1p, 21, and 2p.

Instructions: Listen to the audio and repeat the following sentences. I will say each sentence twice.

1s	ninēhiyawān.	I speak Cree.
2s	kinēhiyawān.	You (sg.) speak Cree.
3s	nēhiyawēw.	S/he speaks Cree.
3's	nēhiyawēyiwa.	His/her _____ (sg.) speaks Cree.
1p	ninēhiyawānān.	We (excl.) speak Cree.
21	kinēhiyawānaw.	We (incl.) speak Cree.
2p	kinēhiyawānāwāw.	You (pl.) speak Cree.
3p	nēhiyawēwak.	They speak Cree.
3'p	nēhiyawēyiwa.	Their _____ (pl.) speak Cree.

Drill 9.2. Conjunct Mode

Instructions: Listen to the audio and repeat the following phrases after me. I will say each one twice.

1s	ē-nēhiyawēyān	as I speak Cree
2s	ē-nēhiyawēyan	as you (sg.) speak Cree
3s	ē-nēhiyawēt	as s/he speaks Cree
3's	ē-nēhiyawēyit	as his/her _____ (sg.) speaks Cree
1p	ē-nēhiyawēyāhk	as we (excl.) speak Cree
21	ē-nēhiyawēyahk	as we (incl.) speak Cree
2p	ē-nēhiyawēyēk	as you (pl.) speak Cree
3p	ē-nēhiyawēcik	as they speak Cree
3'p	ē-nēhiyawēyit	as their ____ (pl.) speak Cree

Remember that when one uses the Conjunct mode, it may be translated as "I am speaking Cree."

Drill 9.3. Review of Sentences

Instructions: Read along as I narrate the following sentences and pay attention to the Cree and English verb forms, especially the suffixes (endings).

1. tānitē minōs **ē-nipāt**?
    Where is the cat **sleeping**?

2. anita sīpā mīcisowināhtikohk māna **nipāw**.
    It usually **sleeps** right there under the table.

3. **ē-nihtā-nēhiyawēt** cī ana iskwēsis?
    Is that little girl **able to speak Cree**?

4. āha, **nihtā-nēhiyawēw**.
    Yes, **she can speak Cree**.

5. **nikī-wāpamāwak** aniki awāsisak **ē-mētawēcik**
    wayawītimihk otākosīhk.
    I saw those children **playing** outside yesterday.

6. tānitahto tipahikan māna **ē-waniskāyan**?
    What time **do you** (sg.) usually **get up**?

Drill 9.4. Questions and Answers

Instructions: Read along as I narrate the following sentences
and pay attention to the Cree and English verb forms.

1. tānitē ē-wī-itohtēyan?
    Where are you intending to go?

2. ōtēnāhk kēhcināc nika-itohtān.
    It is possible that I will go to town.

3. aspin wiyawāw mētawēwikamikohk ē-itohtēcik.
    They're gone to the gym.

4. tāniwā ēkwa wiya kitōtēm?
    Where is your friend?

5. sōniyāwikamikohk.
    At the bank.

6. tāniwēhā kimasinahikana?
    Where are your books?

7. mīcisowināhtikohk astēwa.
    They are on the table.

8. tāniwēhkāk kiskinwahamawākanak?
    Where are the students?

9. āsay ati-kīwēwak.
    They are already on their way home.

Exercise 9.1. Independent and Conjunct Modes

Instructions: Listen as I dictate the verb in the Independent mode on the left side two times, then write each verb in the Conjunct mode in the space provided. Check your answers against the key at the back of the book.

Before we begin this exercise, listen as I say the following three examples. Note that I will *only* be saying the words in the left-hand column. I will *not* be saying the verb in the Conjunct mode, which you will have to write.

Independent Mode		Conjunct Mode
1s	nimīcison	ē-mīcisoyān
1s	ninipān	ē-nipāyān
1s	niwaniskān	ē-waniskāyān

We will now begin the exercise.

Independent Mode		Conjunct Mode
1.	(1s) nipāhpin	_____
2.	(2s) kimīcison	_____
3.	(2s) kinipān	_____
4.	(2s) kiwaniskān	_____

5. (2s) kipāhpin

_____

6. (3s) apiw

_____

7. (3s) ayamihcikēw

_____

8. (3s) masinahikēw

_____

9. (3s) kīwēw

_____

10. (3's) apiyiwa

_____

11. (3's) ayamihcikēyiwa

_____

12. (3's) masinahikēyiwa

_____

13. (3's) kīwēyiwa

_____

14. (1p) nisipwēhtānān

_____

15. (1p) nipimohtānān

_____

16. (1p) nipimipahtānān

_____

17. (1p) nisēsāwipahtānān

_____

18. (21) kisipwēhtānaw

_____

19. (21) kipimohtānaw

_____

20. (21) kipimipahtānaw

_____

21. (21) kisēsāwipahtānaw

_____

22. (2p) kipaminawasonāwāw _____

23. (2p) kikīsitēponāwāw _____

24. (2p) kipahkwēsikanihkānāwāw _____

25. (2p) kinīmānāwāw _____

26. (3p) itohtēwak _____

27. (3p) mētawēwak _____

28. (3p) pāhpiwak _____

29. (3p) pwātisimowak _____

30. (3'p) nakīyiwa _____

31. (3'p) mētawēyiwa _____

32. (3'p) kotawēyiwa _____

Language Lab Session 10

Third Person, Future Conditional, and Vital Statistics

Drill 10.1. Third Person Singular, Plural, and Obviative

Refer to Chapters 11 and 17 for detailed descriptions and information on these third person forms.

Instructions: Listen to the audio and repeat the following sentences. Read along as I narrate the Cree sentences, then underline only the verb stems in each. Notice the suffixes for the third person singular and plural and the obviative. The first sentence is done for you. You may have to listen to these more than once. Check your answers against the key at the back of the book.

Talking about Third Person	Talking about Third Person's Friend
1. cāc awa <u>isiyihkāso</u>w.	hēriy <u>isiyihkāso</u>**yiwa** cāc otōtēma.
This one is named George.	George's friend is called Harry.

2. miywēyihtam cāc.

    George is happy.

    miywēyihtamiyiwa cāc
    otōtēma ēkosi mistahi
    pāhpiyiwa.

    George's friend is happy, so
    he (his friend) laughs a lot.

3. masinahikēw mēriy,
    namōya ayamihcikēw.
    Mary is writing, not
    reading.

    māka wiya otōtēma
    mēriy ayamihcikēyiwa.
    But Mary's friend is reading.

4. cāc ēkwa mēriy
    mīcisowak mēkwāc.
    George and Mary are
    eating right now.

    otōtēmiwāwa mīna
    mīcisoyiwa.
    Their friends are eating also.

5. cāniy mētoni tāhcipow.

    Johnny is very stout/fat.

    otōtēma mīna cāniy
    tāhcipoyiwa.
    Johnny's friend is also
    stout/fat.

Drill 10.2. Future Conditionals

Instructions: Listen as I narrate the following sentences in Cree and repeat after me. I will dictate the present tense first and then move across the row to the Future Conditional example. Observe the changes that occur to the present tense of the inanimate intransitive verb when it is in the Future Conditional form.

For the following drill and exercises, refer to Chapter 14 for a detailed look at the Future Conditional form.

Present Tense	**Future Conditional**
1. wāpan.	wāpahki
It is daylight/morning.	when/if it is daylight/morning

2. kīkisēpāyāw. kīkisēpāyāki
   It is morning. when/if it is morning

3. āpihtā-kīsikāw. āpihtā-kīsikāki
   It is noon. when/if it is noon (at noon)

4. pōn-āpihtā-kīsikāw. pōn-āpihtā-kīsikāki
   It is afternoon. when/if it is afternoon (in
   the/this afternoon)

5. otākosin. otākosiki
   It is late afternoon/ when/if it is late afternoon/
   evening. evening (in the/this evening)

6. tipiskāw. tipiskāki
   It is dark/night. when/if it is dark/night
   (tonight)

Exercise 10.1. Time of Day

Instructions: Listen to the following sentences as I read them and fill in the blanks by translating the English words to Cree. Check your answers against the key at the back of the book.

1. niwī-itohtānān mīcisowikamikohk _____.
   at noon

2. kī-pē-kiyokēwak aniki _____.
   last night

3. kawisimotān ēkwa. _____.
   It is dark/night.

4. pōni-kimiwahki ici kika-mētawānāwāw wayawītimihk

   _____.
                 this evening

5. _____ici kika-sipwēhtānaw.
          When it is daylight

6. wī-nitawi-pakāsimowak awāsisak anohc _____.
                                                this afternoon

Drill 10.3   Miscellaneous Vocabulary

Instructions: Listen to the audio. I will say each Cree word twice, then repeat after me.

wīpac	early/soon
otākosīhk	yesterday
āskaw	sometimes
mwēstas	later
pātimā	later on
āsay	already
kīsowahpison	a scarf
pōsiw.	S/he boards.
mitās	trousers
nikamow.	S/he sings.
namōya wīhkāc	never
namōya cēskwa	not yet
awasotākosīhk	the day before yesterday
namōya pitamā	not for now
wīpacīs	in a little while
apihkēw.	S/he has braids. (hair)

osāwistikwānēw.	S/he has red hair.
kapāw.	S/he comes ashore.
kinwāniskwēw.	S/he has long hair.
asikanak	socks/stockings

Drill 10.4. Vital Statistics

Instructions: Listen as I narrate the following sentences in Cree twice and repeat after me. Take note of the Future Conditional forms of the verbs.

1. pēyak akimihci ohpahowi-pīsim nimis ta-tipiskam.
   My older sister will have a birthday on August 1st.
   My older sister's birthday is August 1st.

2. tānispīhk kiya kā-tipiskaman?
   When is your birthday?

3. kēkā-mitātaht akimihci pāskāwihowi-pīsim.
   On June 9th.

4. tānitahto kīcisānak ihtasiwak?
   How many siblings do you have?

5. nēwo nīcisānak, nisto iskwēsisak ēkwa pēyak nāpēsis.
   My four siblings, three girls and one boy.

6. tānitahtopiponēyan?
   How old are you?

7. nīsitanaw nistosāp nitispīhtisīn.
   I am 23 years old.

Review of the Audio Labs in Cree 100

Drill 11.1. Miscellaneous Vocabulary

Instructions: Listen to the audio. I will say each word twice, then repeat after me.

1.	nāpēw	a man
2.	mitās	a pair of trousers
3.	astis	a mitten
4.	tāpiskākan	a scarf
5.	masinahikanāhtik	a pen
6.	nāpēsis	a boy
7.	iskwēsis	a girl
8.	iskwēw	a woman
9.	astotin	a hat/cap
10.	iskwāhtēm	a door
11.	masinahikan	a book
12.	wāsēnikan	a window
13.	maskisin	a shoe
14.	miskotākay	a coat/dress
15.	mīcisowināhtik	a table

16. masinahikēwināpisk   a chalkboard
17. masinahikēwināhtik   a desk
18. tēhtapiwin   a chair
19. kāsīhikan   a chalkboard brush
20. masinahikēwasiniy   chalk
21. asikan   .a sock

Exercise 11.1. Matching Months

Instructions: Listen to the narration of Cree months in column B. Then match the English translations in column A with the Cree months in column B. The first one is done for you. Check your answers against the key at the back of the book.

A
1. The Budding Moon
2. The Flying Up Moon
3. The Great Moon
4. The Frog Moon
5. The Autumn Moon
6. The Frost-Exploding Trees Moon
7. The Hatching Moon
8. The Goose Moon
9. The Moulting Moon
10. The Frost Moon
11. The Eagle Moon
12. The Migrating Moon

B
a. __7__ pāskāwihowi-pīsim
b. _____ ihkopiwi-pīsim
c. _____ sākipakāwi-pīsim
d. _____ takwāki-pīsim
e. _____ kisē-pīsim
f. _____ ohpahowi-pīsim
g. _____ ayīki-pīsim
h. _____ paskowi-pīsim
i. _____ pawācakinasīsi-pīsim
j. _____ niski-pīsim
k. _____ pimihāwi-pīsim
l. _____ mikisiwi-pīsim

This concludes the Cree 100 language lab sessions.

CREE 101

Language Lab Session 12
Animate Intransitive Verbs (VAI) and Calendar Dates

Drill 12.1. Review of VAI Verb Conjugation

Instructions: Sit with your eyes closed and listen as I conjugate a VAI verb "*api,*" which means "to sit." Do you remember the difference between the Independent and Conjunct modes? Remind yourself of the significance of the numbers, the person indicators, and the placement of the verb stem.

Refer to Chapter 11 for a detailed explanation of the conjugation of animate intransitive verbs.

    I will conjugate the verb "*api*" first in the Independent mode and then in the Conjunct. Repeat after me.

"*api – sit*"

	Independent Mode		Conjunct Mode
1s	nitapin	1s	ē-apiyān
2s	kitapin	2s	ē-apiyan
3s	apiw	3s	ē-apit
3's	apiyiwa	3's	ē-apiyit
1p	nitapinān	1p	ē-apiyāhk
21	kitapinaw	21	ē-apiyahk
2p	kitapināwāw	2p	c̄-apiyc̄k
3p	apiwak	3p	ē-apicik
3'p	apiyiwa	3'p	ē-apiyit

Drill 12.2. Review of Additional Verbs

Instructions: In this second drill, notice that several additional verbs are used to demonstrate the VAI conjugation. I will conjugate the verbs first in the Independent mode and then in the Conjunct. Repeat after me.

You may wish to consult the vocabulary list in your textbook.

Independent Mode		Conjunct Mode	
1s	nimīcison	1s	ē-mīcisoyān
2s	kipāhpin	2s	ē-pāhpiyan
3s	nēhiyawēw	3s	ē-nēhiyawēt
3's	minihkwēyiwa	3's	ē-minihkwēyit
1p	nimīcisonān	1p	ē-mīcisoyāhk
21	kipāhpinaw	21	ē-pāhpiyahk
2p	kinēhiyawānāwāw	2p	ē-nēhiyawēyēk
3p	itohtēwak	3p	ē-itohtēcik
3'p	kīwēyiwa	3'p	ē-kīwēyit

Exercise 12.1. Verb Stems

Instructions: Listen as I narrate the verb stems. Write each verb stem in the spaces provided. Then in the second and third columns, write the inflections (prefixes and suffixes or endings) that mark the Independent and Conjunct modes. Note that I will only narrate the verb stems. The rest of this exercise is written. Check your answers against the key at the back of the book.

Verb Stems	Independent Inflections	Conjunct Inflections
1s _____	_____	_____
2s _____	_____	_____
3s _____	_____	_____
3's _____	_____	_____
1p _____	_____	_____
21 _____	_____	_____
2p _____	_____	_____
3p _____	_____	_____
3'p _____	_____	_____

Dialogue 12.1. Travel

Instructions: This dialogue section has been divided into two parts. The first is a list of vocabulary, which we will dictate. Second, there is a sample conversation phrase using the vocabulary, which we will read. Listen and follow along with the vocabulary and sample phrasing. We will repeat the entire conversation at the end. Afterwards role play the dialogue with a fellow student in the role of Bob or Betty.

1. Vocabulary:	tānitē?	where?
	ē-itohtēyan	as you (sg.) go
	wī-	preverb: Future Intentional

Bob: **tānitē ē-wī-itohtēyan?**
Where are you going?

2. Vocabulary:	mīnisihk	City of Saskatoon
	ispiso	travel by vehicle
	wī-	preverb: Future Intentional
	niwī-ispisonān	we (excl.) are travelling to
	niyānano-kīsikāw	Friday
	niyānano-kīsikāki	when it is Friday
	niya	me/mine
	ēkwa	and

Betty: **niya ēkwa Mary niwī-ispisonān mīnisihk niyāno-kīsikāki.**
Mary and I are going (travelling) to Saskatoon on Friday.

3. Vocabulary:	awīna?	who?
	wī-	preverb: Future Intentional
	wāpam	see him/her
	ēkotē	over there

Bob: **awīna ē-wī-wāpamāyēk ēkotē?**
Who are you going to see there?

4. Vocabulary: nimis   my older sister
                     otōtēma   his/her friend
                     ēkwa   and
                     mīna   also

Betty: **nimis Joan ēkwa mīna Joe, Mary otōtēma.**
My older sister Joan and also Joe, Mary's friend.

5. Vocabulary: ahpō ētikwē   perhaps
                     mīna   also
                     kiyokaw   visit him/her
                     kīspin   if
                     api   be at home
                     nōhkom   my grandmother

Betty: **ahpō ētikwē nika-kiyokawāw nōhkom kīspin apici.**
Perhaps I will visit my grandmother if she's home.

6. Vocabulary: mīciso   eat
                     nitawi-   go and (preverb)
                     nōhtēhkatē   to be hungry
                     cī   question indicator
                     ōma   this (demonstrative pronoun)

Bob: **ē-nitawi-mīcisoyān ōma, kinōhtēhkatān cī?**
I'm going to eat. Are you hungry?

7. Vocabulary: āha   yes
                     tānitē where?
                     māka   but
                     kē-   (preverb) shall
                     mīciso eat

Betty: **āha, tānitē māka kē-mīcisoyahk?**
Yes, where shall we eat?

8. Vocabulary:

piko ita	anywhere (colloquial)
tānitē	where?
kiya	you
nōhtē-	want to
mīciso	eat

Bob: **piko ita, tānitē kiya kinōhtē-mīcison?**
Anywhere. Where do you want to eat?

Betty: **piko ita.**
Anywhere.

Bob: **ahāw.**
Okay.

Conversation without Vocabulary Breakdown

Bob: tānitē ē-wī-itohtēyan?

Betty: niya ēkwa Mary niwī-ispisonān mīnisihk niyāno-kīsikāki.

Bob: awīna ē-wī-wāpamāyēk ēkotē?

Betty: nimis Joan ēwa mīna Joe, Mary otōtēma.
ahpō ētikwē nika-kiyokawāw nōhkom kīspin apici.

Bob: ē-nitawi-mīcisoyān ōma, kinōhtēhkatān cī?

Betty: āha, tānitē māka kē-mīcisoyahk?

Bob: piko ita, tānitē kiya kinōhtē-mīcison?

Betty: piko ita.

Bob: ahāw.

Drill 12.3. Calendar Dates

Instructions: Listen to the audio and repeat the following numbers for calendar dates. I will move across each row, saying the date in the Independent mode first, followed by the Conjunct. First, I will start with the dates from 1 to 10.

Refer to Chapter 15 for more information on the seasons, months, and weekdays. Since there were no weekdays or calendars, the Cree people used the moon to determine the seasons and months. Note that the following numbers are used only for calendar dates. For more information, refer to the dictionary by Arok Wolvengrey, nēhiyawēwin: itwēwina/Cree: Words, Volume 2: English–Cree, page 622.

	Independent Mode	**Conjunct Mode**
1	pēyak akimāw	pēyak ē-akimiht
2	nīso akimāw	nīso ē-akimiht
3	nisto akimāw	nisto ē-akimiht
4	nēwo akimāw	nēwo ē-akimiht
5	niyānan akimāw	niyānan ē-akimiht
6	nikotwāsik akimāw	nikotwāsik ē-akimiht
7	tēpakohp akimāw	tēpakohp ē-akimiht
8	ayēnānēw akimāw	ayēnānēw ē-akimiht
9	kēkā-mitātaht akimāw	kēkā-mitātaht ē-akimiht
10	mitātaht akimāw	mitātaht ē-akimiht

Next, the teen numbers are fairly straightforward. Listen to and repeat after me as I say the following numbers for calendar dates from 11 to 19. I will start with the Independent mode and continue across with the Conjunct mode of the calendar date. Notice there are two ways to say 19.

	Independent Mode	**Conjunct Mode**
11	pēyakosāp akimāw	pēyakosāp ē-akimiht
12	nīsosāp akimāw	nīsosāp ē-akimiht
13	nīstosāp akimāw	nīstosāp ē-akimiht
14	nēwosāp akimāw	nēwosāp ē-akimiht
15	niyānanosāp akimāw	niyānanosāp ē-akimiht
16	nikotwāsosāp akimāw	nikotwāsosāp ē-akimiht
17	tēpakohposāp akimāw	tēpakohposāp ē-akimiht
18	ayēnānēwosāp akimāw	ayēnānēwosāp ē-akimiht

19   kēkā-mitātahtosāp akimāw kēkā-mitātahtosāp
                                ē-akimiht
      (*or* kēkāc-nīsitanaw akimāw) (*or* kēkāc-nīsitanaw
                                ē-akimiht)

Finally, listen and repeat as I say the following numbers for calendar dates from 20 to 31. As above, I will start with the Independent mode and continue across with the Conjunct mode of the calendar date.

	Independent Mode	**Conjunct Mode**
20	nīsitanaw akimāw	nīsitanaw ē-akimiht
21	nīsitanaw-pēyakosāp akimāw	nīsitanaw-pēyakosāp ē-akimiht
22	nīsitanaw-nīsosāp akimāw	nīsitanaw-nīsosāp ē-akimiht
23	nīsitanaw-nistosāp akimāw	nīsitanaw-nistosāp ē-akimiht
24	nīsitanaw-nēwosāp akimāw	nīsitanaw nēwosāp ē-akimiht
25	nīsitanaw-niyānanosāp akimāw	nīsitanaw-niyānanosāp ē-akimiht
26	nīsitanaw-nikotwāsosāp akimāw	nīsitanaw-nikotwāsosāp ē-akimiht
27	nīsitanaw-tēpakohposāp akimāw	nīsitanaw-tēpakohposāp ē-akimiht
28	nīsitanaw-ayēnānēwosāp akimāw	nīsitanaw ayēnānēwosāp ē-akimiht
29	kēkāc-nistomitanaw akimāw	kēkāc-nistomitanaw ē-akimiht
30	nistomitanaw akimāw	nistomitanaw ē-akimiht
31	nistomitanaw-pēyakosāp akimāw	nistomitanaw-pēyakosāp ē-akimiht

Exercise 12.2. Today's Date

Instructions: Listen as I narrate the following question twice, then repeat the question. Provide your own answer with the correct date for today.

tāniyikohk awa pīsim ē-akimiht?
How much is this moon counted? *or* What is the date?

_____

Language Lab Session 13

VAI and VII in Independent and Conjunct Modes and Future Conditional Form, Weather Terms

Drill 13.1. VAI—Singular Actors

For the next two drills, refer to Chapter 11 for a detailed explanation of the conjugation of animate intransitive verbs.

Instructions: The following sentences provide examples of Independent and Conjunct mode singular actors. Listen to the audio and repeat the following sentences. I will say each sentence twice.

Underlining the verb stem and looking at the person indicator and the suffix in each sentence will help you to see who is doing the actions, which are not directed at another person (i.e., intransitive).

1. nitapin tahkohc mīcisowināhtikohk.
   I am sitting on (top of) the table.

2. nīsta ōma ōta ē-apiyān.
   I also am sitting here.

3. kitapin kiya mohcihk.
   You (sg.) are sitting on the ground/floor.

4. ē-wī-apiyan cī kīsta anita?
   Are you (sg.) going to sit there too?

5. apiw cī mēkwāc mēriy?
   Is Mary home right now?

6. ta-apiw cī mēriy tipiskāyiki?
   Will Mary be home tonight? (Literally: Will Mary be
      home when it is dark?)

7. nēhiyawēyiwa cī otōtēma?
   Does his/her friend speak Cree?

8. otēma anihi ē-kī-nipāyit sīpā tēhtapiwinihk.
   His/her dog slept under the chair.

Drill 13.2. VAI—Plural Actors

Instructions: The sentences in this drill show that there is more
than one person involved in the action. Listen to the audio and
repeat the following sentences. I will say each sentence twice.

*Underline the verb
stem and examine
the suffixes. This
will help you to
recognize who is
doing the action.*

1. niwī-kakwē-nisitohtēnān ōma nēhiyawēwin.
   We (excl.) are going to try to understand Cree.

2. kēyāpic ōma ē-wī-kakwē-nisitohtamāhk nēhiyawēwin.
   We (excl.) are still going to try to understand Cree.

3. kiwī-ayamihtānaw ōma ācimowin anohc.
   We (incl.) are going to read this story today.

4. namōya, kotak anima kā-wī-ayamihtāyahk.
   No, it is the other one that we are going to read.

5. nēhiyawasinahikēwin wīpac kika-nihtā-ayamihtānawāw.
   You (pl.) will be able to read Cree soon.

6. āsay cī ē-kī-mīcisoyēk kiyawāw?
   Have you eaten already?

7. kī-itohtēwak ōtēnāhk tipiskohk.
   They went to town last night.

8. ē-kī-itohtēcik cī wīstawāw ēkotē?
   Did they go over there too?

Drill 13.3. VII Conjunct Mode—Weather

For the next drill and exercise, refer to Chapter 14 for a detailed explanation of VII verbs and their use to describe weather in the Conjunct mode and Future Conditional form.

Instructions: Listen carefully as I say each term twice. Repeat after me. The first three examples demonstrate how you can compose a sentence regarding the weather.

1. **ē-wāsēskwahk** ōma, nitawi-mētawētān wayawītimihk.
   It's sunny. Let's go out and play.
      or Let's go and play outside as it is sunny.

2. postastotinē **ē-yōtik** ōma anohc.
   Put on your hat as it is windy today.

3. mētoni **ē-māci-sōhkiyowēk** nikī-pihtokwānān.
   We came inside as it is really starting to be very windy.

Let's begin with the terms.

ē-kimiwahk	as it is raining
ē-kimiwasik	as it is raining a little
ē-sīkipēstāk	as it is pouring (rain)
ē-pahkipēstāk	as it is raining (big drops of rain)
ē-kaskanawipēstāk	as it is misty
ē-yīkwaskwahk	as it is cloudy
ē-yīkowahk	as it is foggy

ē-pīwahk	as it is drifting (snow)
ē-mispok	as it is snowing
ē-āhkwatik	as it is freezing
ē-kisināk	as it is cold
ē-tahkāyāk	as it is cold
ē-kisāstēk	as it is hot (weather)
ē-kisitēk	as it is hot
ē-kīsapwēyāk	as it is a warm day
ē-tihkitēk	as it is melting
ē-saskahk	as it is breaking up
ē-kīsikāk	as it is daytime
ē-miyo-kīsikāk	as it is a nice day
ē-māyi-kīsikāk	as it is not a nice day
ē-tipiskāk	as it is dark/night
ē-nīpāyāstēk	as it is moonlight

Exercise 13.1. Future Conditional Weather Terms

Instructions: Listen carefully as I say each weather term in the Future Conditional form and then repeat after me. I will say each term twice.

Then, in the space below, translate the Future Conditional weather terms into English. Next, write the present tense of these weather terms and again provide the English translation. I will give you a hint: parts of these terms may be familiar from other vocabulary used in previous drills. Check your answers against the key at the back of the book.

1. Future Conditional: wāsēskwahki

   English Translation: _____

   Present Tense Independent: _____

   English Translation: _____

2. Future Conditional: yōtiki

   English Translation: _____

   Present Tense Independent: _____

   English Translation: _____

3. Future Conditional: sōhkiyowēki

   English Translation: _____

   Present Tense Independent: _____

   English Translation: _____

4. Future Conditional: kimiwahki

   English Translation: _____

   Present Tense Independent: _____

   English Translation: _____

5. Future Conditional: sīkipēstāki

   English Translation: _____

   Present Tense Independent: _____

   English Translation: _____

6. Future Conditional: pahkipēstāki

   English Translation: _____

   Present Tense Independent: _____

   English Translation: _____

7. Future Conditional: kaskanawipēstāki

   English Translation: _____

   Present Tense Independent: _____

   English Translation: _____

8. Future Conditional: yīkwaskwahki

   English Translation: _____

   Present Tense Independent: _____

   English Translation: _____

9. Future Conditional: yīkowahki

   English Translation: _____

   Present Tense Independent: _____

   English Translation: _____

10. Future Conditional: pīwahki

   English Translation: _____

   Present Tense Independent: _____

   English Translation: _____

11. Future Conditional: mispoki

   English Translation: _____

   Present Tense Independent: _____

   English Translation: _____

12. Future Conditional: āhkwatiki

    English Translation: _____

    Present Tense Independent: _____

    English Translation: _____

13. Future Conditional: kisināki

    English Translation: _____

    Present Tense Independent: _____

    English Translation: _____

14. Future Conditional: tahkāyāki

    English Translation: _____

    Present Tense Independent: _____

    English Translation: _____

15. Future Conditional: kisāstēki

    English Translation: _____

    Present Tense Independent: _____

    English Translation: _____

16. Future Conditional: kisitēki

    English Translation: _____

    Present Tense Independent: _____

    English Translation: _____

17. Future Conditional: kīsapwēyāki

   English Translation: _____

   Present Tense Independent: _____

   English Translation: _____

18. Future Conditional: tihkitēki

   English Translation: _____

   Present Tense Independent: _____

   English Translation: _____

19. Future Conditional: saskahki

   English Translation: _____

   Present Tense Independent: _____

   English Translation: _____

20. Future Conditional: kimiwasiki

   English Translation: _____

   Present Tense Independent: _____

   English Translation: _____

Transitive Animate Verbs (VTA), Singular and Plural Objects

Drill 14.1. Transitive Animate Verbs with Singular Objects

Refer to Chapters 18 to 21 of the textbook for a detailed explanation of transitive animate verbs (VTA).

Instructions: Listen to the audio and repeat the following transitive animate verbs with singular objects. I will say each word twice.

1s	**ni**pēhtawāw.	I hear him/her/it.
2s	**ki**pēhtawāw.	You (sg.) hear him/her/it.
3s	pēhtaw**ē**w.	He/she/it hears him/her/it.
3's	pēhtaw**ēyiwa**.	His/her _____ (sg.) hears him/her/it.
1p	**ni**nisitohtaw**ānān**.	We understand him/her.
21	**ki**wāpam**ānaw**.	We see him/her/it.
2p	**ki**pāhpih**āwāw**.	You (pl.) laugh at him/her/it.
3p	asam**ēwak**.	They feed him/her/it.
3'p	ohpin**ēyiwa**.	His/her _____ (pl.) lift him/her/it.

Drill 14.2. More Transitive Animate Verbs with Singular Objects

Instructions: Listen as I dictate the following sentences. Then repeat after me. Listen carefully to the pronunciation of the verb as spoken where the object is seen, heard, or fed. Ask yourself: Is the object singular? Is it also performing an action? The translation will help you to understand the verb construction.

1. **ni**pēhtaw**āw** piyēsīs ē-nikamot.
    I hear a bird singing.

2. **ki**pēhtaw**āw** cī kīsta?
    Do you (sg.) hear it too?

3. Johnny wīsta pēhtaw**ēw** piyēsīsa ē-nikamoyit.
    Johnny hears the bird singing too.

4. omisa asam**ēyiwa** atimwa.
    His/her sister feeds the dog.

5. **ni**nisitohtaw**ānān** kiskinwahamākēw āskaw.
    We (excl.) understand the teacher sometimes.

6. **ki**ka-wāpam**ānaw** ici wīpac.
    We (incl.) will see him/her soon.

7. **ki**kī-pāhpih**āwāw** cī ana ē-mōhcohkāsot?
    Did you (pl.) laugh at him/her when he/she was
       acting silly?

8. kī-asam**ēwak** awāsisa.
    They fed the child.

9. ostēsa kī-ohpin**ēyiwa** anihi mītosa.
    His/her brother lifted the tree.

Drill 14.3. Transitive Animate Verbs with Plural Objects

Note that these verbs have almost the same form, except that some add the suffix "-ak" (as underlined) to indicate a plural object.

Instructions: Listen as I say the following sentences. I will say each sentence twice. Then repeat after me.

1s	**ni**wīsāmā**wak**.	I invite them.
2s	**ki**wāpamā**wak**.	You (sg.) see them.
3s	wīcēwēw.	He/she accompanies them.
3's	wīcēwēyiwa.	His/her ____ (sg.) accompanies them.
1p	**ni**pāhpihānā**nak**.	We (excl.) laugh at them.
21	**ki**kiyokawā**nawak**.	We (incl.) visit them.
2p	**ki**wīsāmā**wāwak**.	You (pl.) invite them.
3p	pēhtawēw.	They hear them.
3'p	kiyokawēyiwa.	His/her ___ (pl.) visit them.

Drill 14.4. More Transitive Animate Verbs with Plural Objects

This part of your lab session gives you an opportunity to practise talking about hearing, feeding, seeing, and lifting more than one object. One can apply these verbs to interactions with family, friends, or pets.

Instructions: Listen as I say the following sentences. Repeat after me. I will say each sentence twice.

1. **ni**pēhtawā**wak** piyēsīsak ē-nikamocik.
   I hear the birds singing.

2. **ki**pēhtawā**wak** cī kīsta?
   Do you (sg.) hear them too?

3. Johnny pēhtawēw wīsta.
   Johnny hears them too.

4. omisa asamēyiwa atimwa.
   His/her sisters feeds the dogs.

5. **ni**nisitohtaw**ānānak** āskaw kiskinwahamākēwak.
   We (excl.) understand the teachers sometimes.

6. **ki**ka-wāpam**ānawak** sīsīpak sākahikanihk.
   We (incl.) will see the ducks at the lake.

7. **ki**kī-pāhpih**āwāwak** cī aniki ē-mōhcohkāsocik?
   Did you (pl.) laugh at them when they were acting silly?

8. kī-asam**ēwak** kahkiyaw awāsisa.
   They fed all the children.

9. ostēsa kī-ohpin**ēyiwa** anihi mītosa.
   His/her brothers lifted the trees.

Dialogue 14.1. Visiting Friends

Instructions: Listen to the following dialogue illustrating a conversation between two friends. The dialogue will be repeated twice. Then practise the dialogue with a partner.

Betty: **tānisi ēkwa kiya, nitōtēm?**
                    How are you, my friend?

Darren: **namōya nānitaw. tānitē ē-ohtohtēyan?**
                    Fine. Where are you coming (arriving) from?

Betty: **pīt ē-kī-nitawi-wāpamak māka namōya apiw.**
                    I went to see Pete, but he's not at home.

Darren: **aspin ana ē-kī-nitawi-kiyokēt iskonikanihk. ahpō ētikwē**
                    kī kapēsiw ēkotē.
                    He went to visit at the reserve. Perhaps he stayed (camped)
                    overnight out there.

Betty:	**pīhtokwēk. nikī-nihtīhkān.** Come in. I made tea.
Darren:	**ahāw.** Okay.
Betty:	**ahāw.** Okay.

Language Lab Session 15

Possessive Form for Singular Animate Nouns, Kinship Terms, and Interrogative Pronouns

Drill 15.1. Possessive Form for Singular Animate Nouns

Instructions: Listen as I conjugate the noun "*sīsīp*," which means "duck." I will say each conjugated form twice, then repeat after me. Notice the special suffix "*-im*," which is added to some nouns before all regular suffixes.

Refer to Chapter 31 for a detailed explanation of the possessive and how it is formed.

"*sīsīp* – duck"

1s	**nisīsīpim**	my duck
2s	**kisīsīpim**	your (sg.) duck
3s	**osīsīpima**	his/her duck
3's	**osīsīpimiyiwa**	his/her _____'s (sg.) duck
1p	**nisīsīpiminān**	our (excl.) duck
21	**kisīsīpiminaw**	our (incl.) duck
2p	**kisīsīpimiwāw**	your (pl.) duck
3p	**osīsīpimiwāwa**	their duck
3'p	**osīsīpimiyiwa**	their _____s' (pl.) duck

Drill 15.2. Possessive of *atim/misatim*

Instructions: Listen as I say the following words. I will say each conjugation twice, then repeat after me. Notice that these are irregular possessive forms used to refer to either a dog (*atim*) or a horse (*misatim*). To pluralize you can add "*-ak*" to the first person (1s, 1p) or second person (2s, 2p, 21) forms only. Add "*-a*" to third person forms (3s, 3p).

"atim – dog" / "misatim – horse"

1s	**ni**tēm	my dog/horse
2s	**ki**tēm	your (sg.) dog/horse
3s	**o**tēma	his/her dog/horse
3's	**o**tēm**iyiwa**	his/her _____'s (sg.) dog/horse
1p	**ni**tēm**inān**	our (excl.) dog/horse
21	**ki**tēm**inaw**	our (incl.) dog/horse
2p	**ki**tēm**iwāw**	your (pl.) dog/horse
3p	**o**tēm**iwāwa**	their dog/horse
3'p	**o**tēm**iyiwa**	their _____s' (pl.) dog/horse

Drill 15.3. Possessive of *-nāpēm-*

Instructions: Listen as I conjugate the word "*-nāpēm-*," which means "husband." I will say each conjugation twice, then repeat after me. Note that the change in the Cree word for "man" (*nāpēw*) to mean "husband" includes a form of the "*-im*" suffix.

"-nāpēm- – husband"

1s	**ni**nāpēm	my man/husband
2s	**ki**nāpēm	your (sg.) man/husband
3s	**o**nāpēma	her man/husband

3's	o**nāpēm**iyiwa	her/his_____'s (sg.) man/ husband
1p	ni**nāpēm**inānak	our (excl.) men/husbands
21	ki**nāpēm**inawak	our (incl.) men/husbands
2p	ki**nāpēm**iwāwak	your (pl.) men/husbands
3p	o**nāpēm**iwāwa	their men/husbands
3'p	o**nāpēm**iyiwa	their _____s' (pl.) men/ husbands

Drill 15.4   Kinship Terms

Instructions: Listen as I conjugate the word "-*mosōm*-," which means "grandfather" or "grandpa." I will say the conjugated word twice, then repeat after me.

"-*mosōm*- – grandfather/grandpa"

1s	**ni**mosōm	my grandfather
2s	**ki**mosōm	your (sg.) grandfather
3s	**o**mosōma	his/her grandfather
3's	**o**mosōm**iyiwa**	his/her _____'s (sg.) grandfather
1p	**ni**mosōm**inān**	our (excl.) grandfather
21	**ki**mosōm**inaw**	our (incl.) grandfather
2p	**ki**mosōm**iwāw**	your (pl.) grandfather
3p	**o**mosōm**iwāwa**	their grandfather
3'p	**o**mosōm**iyiwa**	their _____s' (pl.) grandfather

Notice that only 1P, 21, and 2P require the additional suffix "-ak" to show the plural form "men/husbands"; otherwise, the translation would read "our man/ husband," etc. Another noun that follows this pattern is the word "īskwēw," which means "woman." It requires a connective "t" with all of the prefixes (e.g.: "nitiskwēm – my wife").

Notice that all the kinship terms have their unique forms and must be learned as they appear.

Drill 15.5. Review of Possessives, Interrogative Pronouns, Kinship Terms, Tense, and Preverbs

You may wish to consult your textbook on one or all of these topics in this drill.

Instructions: Listen as I say the following sentences. I will say each sentence twice, then repeat after me.

1. tāniwā **ki**sīsīpim?
   Where is your (sg.) duck?

2. tānitē **ki**tēm**iwāw** ē-nipāt?
   Where is your (pl.) dog sleeping?

3. **o**nāpēma cī apiyiwa?
   Is her husband home?

4. **ni**mosōm**inān** wī-pē-kiyokēw.
   Our grandfather is coming to visit.

5. wīpac ōma ēkwa ta-kī-takosihk.
   kika-wīci-mīcisōmikonaw.
   He should be arriving soon. He will eat with us.

6. **o**mosōm**iwāwa** kī-kiyokawēwak otākosīhk.
   They visited their grandfather yesterday.

Exercise 15.1. Dictation and Translation

Instructions: Listen as I dictate ten Cree words. I will say each word twice, then write each word in the spaces below and translate them in the right-hand column. Check your answers against the key at the back of the book.

Dictation   **Translation**

1. _____   _____

2. _____   _____

3. _____   _____

4. _____   _____

5. _____   _____

6. _____   _____

7. _____   _____

8. _____   _____

9. _____   _____

10. _____   _____

Exercise 15.2. Possessive Form

Instructions: Listen as I dictate the following words in the left-hand column. In the space provided, write the appropriate possessive form for the following words. I have completed the first one for you. Check your answers against the key at the back of the book.

1. atim, niya   *e.g.:* nitēm _____

2. atim, wiya   _____

3. mosōm, kiya   _____

4. asikan, niya   _____

5. nāpēw, niya   _____

6. iskwēw, kiya   _____

7. astotin, wiya   _____

Language Lab Session 16
Transitive Inanimate Verbs

Drill 16.1. VTI-1

Instructions: Listen as I conjugate the verb "*pēhta*," which means "to hear it." I will say each conjugated form twice, then repeat after me.

Refer to Chapter 17 for a detailed overview of transitive inanimate verbs (VTI) and their conjugation.

VTI-1 *"pēhta – hear it"*

1s	**ni**pēht**ēn**.	I hear it.
2s	**ki**pēht**ēn**.	You (sg.) hear it.
3s	pēht**am**.	He/she/it hears it.
3's	pēht**amiyiwa**.	His/her/its ____'s (sg.) hears it.
1p	**ni**pēht**ēnān**.	We (excl.) hear it.
21	**ki**pēht**ēnaw**.	We (incl.) hear it.
2p	**ki**pēht**ēnāwāw**.	You (pl.) hear it.
3p	pēht**amwak**.	They hear it.
3'p	pēht**amiyiwa**.	His/her/its ____s' (pl.) hears it.

Recall the rule for conjugating VTI-1 verbs: drop the "a" from the 2s Imperative verb form. Place that in the slot between the person indicator and the ending.

Other VTI-1 include:

nisitohta	understand it	postiska	put in on (clothing)
wāpahta	see it	natona	look for it

Drill 16.2. VTI-1 in Sentences

Instructions: Listen as I say the following sentences and repeat after me.

1. **ni**pēht**ēn** kitohcikan.
   I hear the musical instrument.

2. **ki**kī-pēht**ēn** cī ē-kimiwahk tipiskohk?
   Did you (sg.) hear it raining last night?

3. kī-pēht**am** cī wīsta kā-kimiwaniyik tipiskohk?
   Did he/she hear it raining last night too?

4. omosōmiyiwa wī-nāt**amiyiwa** anihi masinahikana.
   His/her grandfather is going for those books.

5. **ni**ka-masinah**ēnān** niwīhowināna anita
   masinahikanihk.
   We will write our names on that paper.

Exercise 16.1. VTI-1

Instructions: Listen as I narrate the following sentences, then fill in the blanks with the appropriate form of a VTI-1. I will say each sentence twice. Check your answers against the key at the back of the book.

1. _____ otastotiniwāwa.
   They put on their hats.

2. John ēkwa Mary _____ otastotiniwāwa wīstawāw.
   John and Mary **put on** their hats too.

3. _____ kimaskisina sīpā tēhtapiwinihk.
   I saw your (sg.) shoes under the chair.

4. _____ kimaskisina, ēkāwiya māto.
   We (incl.) will look for your shoes, don't cry.

5. _____ cī ōma kīkwāy kā-itwēhk?
   Do you (sg.) understand what is being said?

Drill 16.3. VTI-2

Instructions: Listen as I conjugate the verb "*pimohtatā*," which means "take it along." I will say each conjugated form twice, then repeat after me.

Recall that VTI-2 are conjugated like VAI. Consult Chapter 17 where this particular verb form is discussed.

VTI-2 *"pimohtatā – take it along"*

1s	**ni**pimohtatā**n**.	I take it along.
2s	**ki**pimohtatā**n**.	You (sg.) take it along.
3s	pimohtatā**w**.	He/she takes it along.
3's	pimohtatā**yiwa**.	His/her ____ (sg.) takes it along.
1p	**ni**pimohtatā**nān**.	We (excl.) take it along.
21	**ki**pimohtatā**naw**.	We (incl.) take it along.
2p	**ki**pimohtatā**nāwāw**.	You (pl.) take it along.
3p	pimohtatā**wak**.	They take it along.
3'p	pimohtatā**yiwa**.	His/her ____ (pl.) take it along.

Other VTI-2 include:

āpacihtā	use it	osīhtā	make it
kātā	hide it	pētā	bring it
wanihtā	lose it	kitā	eat all of it
ayamihtā	read it	ayā	have it

Exercise 16.2. VTI-2

Instructions: Listen as I narrate the following sentences. I will say each sentence twice, then fill in the blanks with the appropriate form of a VTI-2. Check your answers against the key at the back of the book.

1. _____ nitastotin anohc. wī-kisāstēw.
   I will take (it) my hat today. It's going to be hot.

2. ocīmānimiwāw _____ sākahikanihk
   itohtētwāwi.
   They will take (it) their canoe along if they go to the lake.

3. nimaskisina cī āsay _____?
   Did you finish my moccasins?

4. John _____ nitastotin.
   John **hid** my hat.

5. nīstanān _____ anihi masinahikana.
   We (excl.) **will use** those books too.

Drill 16.4. VTI-3

You will recall that there are three forms of the verb "eat." The "mīci" form is used to refer to eating foods that are of the inanimate noun category.

Instructions: Listen as I conjugate the verb *"mīci,"* which means "eat it." I will say each conjugated form twice, then repeat after me.

VTI-3 *"mīci – eat it"*

1s	**ni**mīcin.	I eat it. (refers to inanimate nouns)
2s	**ki**mīcin.	You (sg.) eat it.
3s	mīciw.	He/she/it eats it.

3's	**mīci**y**iwa.**	His/her/its _____ (sg.) eats it.
1p	**nimīcinān.**	We (excl.) eat it.
21	**ki**mīci**naw.**	We (incl.) eat it.
2p	**ki**mīci**nāwāw.**	You (pl.) eat it.
3p	mīci**wak.**	They eat it.
3'p	**mīci**y**iwa.**	His/her/its _____ (pl.) eats it.

Exercise 16.3. Fill in the Blank

Instructions: Listen as I narrate the following sentences twice, then fill in the blanks with the appropriate verb, person, and tense. Check your answers against the key at the back of the book.

1. _____ anima mīcimāpoy.
   I ate that soup.

2. _____ anihi masinahikana.
   They lost their books.

3. _____ cī ātiht kocawākanisa?
   Do you have some matches?

4. _____ cī kitastotin?
   Did you (sg.) lose your cap?

5. _____ anihi nīso masinahikana tipiskohk.
   We (excl.) read those two books last night.

Language Lab Session 17
Conjunct Mode

*Refer to Chapter 32 of the textbook for a detailed explanation of the
Conjunct mode.*

Exercise 17.1. Verbs in a Text

Instructions: In the following paragraph, identify the verb stems by
drawing a box around each of them. There are eleven. Then listen to the
recording while you read the paragraph. Check your answers against
the key at the back of the book.

nikī-waniskān wīpac kīkisēp. wayawītimihk mētoni ē-tahkāyāk

ēkosi namōya ninōhtē-itohtān kihci-ōtēnāhk māka ē-kīsi-mīcisoyān

nikī-wayawīn. āta ē-tahkāyāk kī-wāsēskwan. mihcēt piyēsīsak

nikī-wāpamāwak ē-nikamocik mītosihk. nitēm nikī-wīcēwik.

kī-papāmipahtāw misiwē mēskanāhk.

Exercise 17.2. Conjunct Mode—
Past and Future Intentional

Instructions: Listen as I narrate the following sentences, first in the past tense and then in the Future Intentional form. Identify all the verb stems by drawing a box around each of them. I will say each sentence twice. Check your answers against the key at the back of the book.

1. ē-kī-itohtēyān sākahikanihk ēkosi namōya nikī-wāpamāwak.
    I went to the lake, so I didn't see them.

    ē-wī-itohtēyān ōma sākahikanihk wāpahki.
    I'm going to the lake tomorrow.

2. ē-kī-mīcisoyan cī āsay kīsta?
    Did you eat already too?

    mwēstas cī kīsta ē-wī-mīcisoyan?
    Are you going to eat later too?

3. ē-kī-wīcēwāt cī John omosōma?
    Did John go with his grandfather?

    omosōma cī ē-wī-wīcēwāt?
    Is he/she going with/accompanying his/her grandfather?

4. ē-kī-kiyokākoyāhk ana kisēyiniw tipiskohk.
    That old man visited us last night.

    ē-wī-wīcēwikoyāhk awa ōtēnāhk itohtēyāhki.
    He/she is going with us if we go to town.

Exercise 17.3. Dictation Practice

Instructions: Listen carefully to the audio. I will dictate six Cree words. Write each word in the spaces below. Remember you can and should replay the audio so you can decipher the sounds. Check your answers against the key at the back of the book.

1. _____

2. _____

3. _____

4. _____

5. _____

6. _____

Dialogue 17.1. Conversation with Family

Instructions: Listen to the following dialogue illustrating a conversation between a grandmother and her grandchild who has come to visit her. The dialogue will be repeated twice. Then practise the dialogue with a classmate.

Bob: **tānisi, nōhkom?**
How are you, grandma?

ohkoma: **namōya nānitaw, nōsisim. kiya māka, kimiyomahcihon cī ēkwa?**
I'm fine, grandchild. And you? Are you feeling well now?

Bob: **āha, nimiyomahcihon ēkwa māka nisīmisak kēyāpic āhkosiwak.**
Yes, I am feeling better/well now, but my brothers/sisters are still sick.

nah, nimāmā ē-kī-pahkwēsikanihkēt kīkisēp.
Here, my mom baked bannock this morning.

ohkoma: **āy, nitatamihik. api, nika-nihtīhkān.**
Thanks, she pleases me. Sit down, I'll make tea.

kika-mōwānaw awa pahkwēsikan mēkwāc kēyāpic ē-kisisot.
We'll eat this bannock while it is still warm.

Bob: **tāniwā nimosōm?**
Where is my grandfather?

ohkoma: **aspin kistikānihk ē-kī-nitawi-ātoskēt.**
He went to work in the field.

**wīpac ōma ēkwa ta-kī-takosihk.
kika-wīci-mīcisōmikonaw.**
He should be arriving soon now. He will eat with us.

Language Lab Session 18

Inverse Form and VTA with Plural Objects

Drill 18.1. VTA Direct and Inverse

Review Chapters 23 to 26 for a detailed explanation of the Inverse form.

Instructions: Listen as I narrate the following VTA verbs and note the alternation of the endings in the Independent Direct and Inverse forms. I will say the Direct form of the VTA verb and then move across the row and say the Inverse form. I will say each row twice, then repeat after me.

	Direct	**Inverse**
1s	niwāpam**ā**w.	niwāpam**ik**.
	I see him/her.	He/she/it sees me.
2s	kiwāpam**ā**w.	kiwāpam**ik**.
	You see him/her/it.	He/she/it sees you.
3s	wāpam**ē**w.	wāpam**ikow**.
	He/she sees him/her/it.	He/she/it is seen by him/her.
3's	wāpam**ēyiwa**.	wāpam**ikoyiwa**.
	His/her ____ (sg.) sees him/her.	His/her ____ (sg.) is seen by him/her.

1p	niwīcēw**ānān**.	niwīcēw**ikonān**.
	We accompany him/her.	He/she accompanies us.
21	kikiskēyim**ānaw**.	kikiskēyim**ikonaw**.
	We know him/her.	He/she knows us.
2p	kipāhpih**āwāw**.	kipāhpih**ikowāw**.
	You (pl.) laugh at him/her.	He/she laughs at you. (pl.)
3p	wīsām**ēwak**.	wīsām**ikowak**.
	They invite him/her.	They are invited by him/her.
3'p	kakwēcim**ēyiwa**.	kakwēcim**ikoyiwa**.
	His/her ___ (pl.) asks him/her.	His/her ____ (pl.) was asked by him/her.

Drill 18.2. VTA Direct and Inverse in Sentences

Instructions: Listen as I narrate the following sentences, then repeat after me. I will say each sentence twice. Pay attention to the person indicators and the verb stems' suffixes.

1. niwī-wīsāmāw nisīmis atāwēwikamikohk
   ta-itohtēyāhk.
   I'm going to invite my younger brother/sister to go
      to the store.

2. nikī-wīsāmik nimis atāwēwikamikohk ē-wī-itohtēt.
   My older sister invited me along as she is intending
      to go to the store.

3. kī-wāpamēw cī otōtēma tipiskohk?
   Did he/she see his/her friend last night?

4. kī-wāpamikow cī otōtēma?
   Was he/she seen by his/her friend?

5. kinōhtē-kakwēcimāwāw cī kīkway kimosōmiwāw?
    Do you (pl.) want to ask your (pl.) grandfather
        something?

6. kimosōmiwāw kinōhtē-kakwēcimikowāw kīkway.
    Your (pl.) grandfather wants to ask you (pl.)
        something.

Drill 18.3. Transitive Animate Verbs and Plural Objects

Refer to Chapters 18 to 21 of the textbook for a full review of transitive animate verbs.

Instructions: Listen as I narrate the following sentences, then repeat after me. I will say each sentence twice. As you listen to the examples, note the plural endings, which are marked in bold font below.

1. nikī-wāpamāw**ak** awāsis**ak** ē-mētawē**cik**.
    I saw the children playing.

2. kikī-asamāw**ak** cī āsay pāhkahāhkwān**ak**?
    Did you feed the chickens yet?

3. nika-nitawi-kiyokawānān**ak** nitōtēminān**ak**.
    We (excl.) will go and visit our friends.

4. kika-kakwē-asamānaw**ak** wīpac.
        wī-kīwē**wak** ōki anohc.
    We (incl.) will try to serve them a meal soon.
        They are going home today. (Literally: try to feed)

5. nitawāsimis**ak** cī kikī-wāpamāwāw**ak** ē-nīmihitocik?
    Did you (pl.) see my children dancing?

Language Lab Session 19
Time

Drill 19.1. On the Hour

Instructions: Listen as I narrate the sentences below expressing time. I will repeat each sentence twice, then repeat after
me. Keep in mind that the word *"ispayin"* changes with the
different tenses. I will start with the *present* tense.

*For these drills,
refer to Chapter
15 for a detailed
review of seasons,
months, weekdays,
and time. Although
the references
in the textbook
to "clock" time
are minimal, one
can tell time by
following that
description.*

Present Tense

1. pēyak tipahikan **ispayin**.
   It is one o'clock.

2. nīso tipahikan **ispayin**.
   It is two o'clock.

3. nisto tipahikan **ispayin**.
   It is three o'clock.

4. nēwo tipahikan **ispayin**.
   It is four o'clock.

5. niyānan tipahikan **ispayin**.
   It is five o'clock.

6. nikotwāsik tipahikan **ispayin**.
   It is six o'clock.

Now I will narrate time in the Future Conditional form.

Future Conditional

7. tēpakohp tipahikan **ispayiki**...
When it is seven o'clock...

8. ayēnānēw tipahikan **ispayiki**...
When it is eight o'clock...

9. kēkā-mitātaht tipahikan **ispayiki**...
When it is nine o'clock...

10. mitātaht tipahikan **ispayiki**...
When it is ten o'clock...

11. pēyakosāp tipahikan **ispayiki**...
When it is eleven o'clock...

12. nīsosāp tipahikan **ispayiki**...
When it is twelve o'clock...

Drill 19.2. On the Half-Hour

Instructions: Listen as I narrate each sentence below expressing time on the half-hour. I will repeat each sentence twice, then repeat after me. Note that "*mīna āpihtaw*," which can mean "also half," is used to indicate the half-hour.

1. pēyak tipahikan mīna āpihtaw ispayin.
   It is 1:30.

2. nīso tipahikan mīna āpihtaw ispayin.
   It is 2:30.

3. nisto tipahikan mīna āpihtaw ispayin.
   It is 3:30.

4. nēwo tipahikan mīna āpihtaw ispayin.
   It is 4:30.

5. niyānan tipahikan mīna āpihtaw ispayin.
   It is 5:30.

6. nikotwāsik tipahikan mīna āpihtaw ispayin.
   It is 6:30.

Dialogue 19.1. Talking about Time

Instructions: Listen to the following dialogue, illustrating a conversation about time. The dialogue will be repeated twice. Then practise the dialogue with a classmate. Note the brackets ( ) are meant to show optional material. .

Solomon: **tānitahto tipahikan ōma (ē-ispayik mēkwāc)?**
What time is it (right now)?

Mrs. Bear: **nēwo tipahikan (ispayin mēkwāc).**
It is four o'clock (right now).

wīpac ēkwa kisīmisak ta-takohtēwak.
Your younger brothers and sisters will be arriving soon.

Solomon: **sōskwāc cī kika-ati-mīcisonaw takohtētwāwi?**
Will we (incl.) be eating as soon as they arrive?

Mrs. Bear: **āha, ayisk Bobbi ēkwa Joseph wī-nitawi-pwātisimowak otākosiki.**
Yes, because Bobbi and Joseph are going to dance pow-wow this evening.

Solomon: **tānispīhk ē-wī-sipwēhtēyēk?**
When are you (pl.) leaving?

Mrs. Bear: **nānitaw nikotwāsik mīna āpihtaw tipahikan ispayiki.**
When it is about 6:30.

Solomon: **kika-wīcēwitināwāw.**
I will go with you. (pl.)

Mrs. Bear: **namōya, kita-kanawēyimāwasoyan ōma kiya, kisīmisak ōki.**
No, you will babysit your younger siblings (brothers and sisters).

Drill 19.3. Month and Date

Instructions: This short drill is a reminder of how one would ask somebody about the month and date. Listen carefully as I narrate the questions and answers below, then you can practise with a partner. I will say each question and answer twice.

1. Q. **tāna ēwako pīsim?**
   What month (moon) is it?
   A. **takwāki-pīsim mēkwāc.**
   It is September.

2. Q. **tāniyikohk ē-akimiht ēwako pīsim?**
   What date is it?
   A. **nisto akimāw.**
   It is the third.

Drill 19.4 Months

Instructions: Listen as I narrate the names of the months below in Cree. I will say each month twice, then repeat after me. Note that there are two different ways to say "September." After listening to this list of months, select the month when your birthday occurs.

kisē-pīsim	January—The Great Moon
mikisiwi-pīsim	February—The Eagle Moon
niski-pīsim	March—The Goose Moon
ayīki-pīsim	April—The Frog Moon
sākipakāwi-pīsim	May—The Budding Moon
pāskāwihowi-pīsim	June—The Hatching Moon
paskowi-pīsim	July—The Moulting Moon
ohpahowi-pīsim	August—The Flying Up Moon

nōcihitowi-pīsim	September—The Mating Moon
takwāki-pīsim	(*or*) —The Autumn Moon
pimihāwi-pīsim	October—The Migrating Moon
ihkopiwi-pīsim	November—The Frost Moon
pawācakinasīsi-pīsim	December—The Frost-Exploding Trees Moon

Language Lab Session 20
Reflexive Forms

Drill 20.1. Independent Mode Reflexive

Instructions: Listen as I conjugate the VTA verb "*tipēyim*," which means "be in charge of him/her," in the Reflexive form. Note that when a VTA verb stem is written in the Reflexive form, it follows the VAI conjugation chart. The VTA form of the verb "*tipēyim*," which means "be in charge of him/her," changes to "*tipēyimiso*" meaning to "be in charge of oneself" in the Reflexive form.

Refer to Chapter 29 for details on the Reflexive form of verbs.

I will say the conjugation twice, then repeat after me.

VTA "*tipēyim* – be in charge of him/her" /
VAI (Reflexive) "*tipēyimiso* – be in charge of oneself"

1s	ni**tipēyimiso**n.	I am in charge of myself.
2s	ki**tipēyimiso**n.	You (sg.) are in charge of yourself.
3s	**tipēyimiso**w.	He/she is in charge of him/herself.
3's	**tipēyimiso**yiwa.	His/her _____ (sg.) is in charge of him/herself.

— 125 —

1p	ni**tipēyimiso**nān.	We (excl.) are in charge of ourselves.
21	ki**tipēyimiso**naw.	We (incl.) are in charge of ourselves.
2p	ki**tipēyimiso**nāwāw.	You (pl.) are in charge of yourselves.
3p	**tipēyimiso**wak.	They are in charge of themselves.
3'p	**tipēyimiso**yiwa.	His/her _____ (pl.) are in charge of themselves.

Other verbs which follow this conjugation include:

kisīpēkiniso	bathe oneself
asamiso	feed oneself
wīcihiso	help oneself
minahiso	give oneself a drink

Drill 20.2. Conjunct Mode Reflexive

Instructions: Listen as I conjugate the VTA verb *"asamiso,"* which means "to feed oneself." Again, notice that the Reflexive form of the verb follows the VAI conjugation chart. I will say the conjugated verb twice, then repeat after me.

"asamiso – to feed oneself"

1s	ē-**asamiso**yān	as I feed myself
2s	ē-**asamiso**yan	as you (sg.) feed yourself
3s	ē-**asamiso**t	as he/she feeds himself/herself
3's	ē-**asamiso**yit	as his/her _____ (sg.) feeds him/herself
1p	ē-**asamiso**yāhk	as we (excl.) feed ourselves
21	ē-**asamiso**yahk	as we (incl.) feed ourselves
2p	ē-**asamiso**yēk	as you (pl.) feed yourselves
3p	ē-**asamiso**cik	as they feed themselves
3'p	ē-**asamiso**yit	as his/her _____ (pl.) feed themselves

Drill 20.3. Reflexives in Sentences

Instructions: Listen carefully as I narrate the following sentences in Cree. I will say each sentence twice, then repeat after me. Notice that the Reflexive verbs ending in "*-iso*" and "*-āso*" mean "doing [something] for oneself."

1. kika-tipēyim**iso**n kīsihtāyani
   ē-kiskinwahamākawiyan.
   You will be in charge of yourself when you finish
       your education. *or*
   You will be on your own when you finish school.

2. nihtā-asam**iso**wak nicawāsimak āta ē-apisīsisicik.
   My children can feed themselves although they are little.

3. kipēpīm cī āsay nihtā-minah**iso**w?
   Can your baby already give himself a drink?

4. āha, miciminam**āso**w māna minihkwācikanis.
   Yes, he usually holds the cup for himself.

Drill 20.4. Questions and Answers

Instructions: Follow the example and answer the questions. I will dictate the question, pause for you to write the answer, and then repeat the question again and provide the correct answer, which you will repeat after me. Check your answers against the key at the back of the book.

Listen as I narrate the example:

Q: **kikī**-ayamihtān cī pēyak masinahikan?
A: āha, **nikī**-ayamihtān masinahikan.

Let's begin the drill. Notice that some of the sentences are in the past tense.

1. Q: **kikī**-ayamihtān cī pēyak masinahikan?

    A: _____

2. Q: **kikī**-miskēn cī astotin?

    A: _____

3. Q: kinisitohtēn cī nēhiyawēwin?

    A: _____

4. Q: kinōhtē-mīcin cī askipwāwa?

    A: _____

5. Q: **kikī**-yōhtēnēn cī wāsēnikan?

    A: _____

6. Q: kiwāpahtēn cī atāwēwikamik?

    A: _____

7. Q: kitayān cī oyākan?

    A: _____

Cree: Language of the Plains ● Jean L. Okimāsis

Exercise 20.1. Complete the Sentences

Instructions: Listen carefully as I narrate the partial sentences below. I will pause after each sentence to give you time to circle the right noun to complete the sentence. I will then narrate the full sentence and pause for you to repeat after me. Check your answers against the key at the back of the book.

1. wīpac cī kika-pētān (awāsis, masinahikan).

2. kikiskēyimāw cī ana (oskinīkiskwēw, astis).

3. māskōc kika-wāpahtēnāwāw (sākahikan, pahkwēsikan).

4. tāpwē ninōhtē-ayamihānān (astotin, nikāwīnān).

5. namōya nikī-wāpamāw anohc (cīmān, acimosis).

This concludes the Cree 101 language lab sessions.

Answer Key

Cree 100

Language Lab Session 1

Spelling 1.1 (page 5)

1. pakān
2. pahkān
3. asām
4. asam
5. kisistēw
6. kīsitēw
7. sakahikan
8. sākahikan
9. niyānan
10. niyanān

Language Lab Session 2

Spelling 2.1 (page 14)

1. apisīs
2. kiya
3. cīki
4. ēkosi
5. nēwo
6. minōs
7. iskwēw
8. wāwa
9. mitōn
10. miskāt
11. tānisi
12. nīpin
13. māka
14. sōniyāw
15. mēkwāc
16. atim
17. kinēpikos
18. akohp
19. tēhtapiwin
20. misit

Language Lab Session 3

Spelling 3.1 (page 18)

1. maskwa
2. nitōtēm
3. ospwākan
4. tohtōsāpoy
5. pēyak
6. cēskwa
7. asiniy
8. acimosis
9. masinahikan
10. wāhyaw
11. maskosis
12. sikākwak
13. mispiton
14. ayinānēw

Drill 3.4 (page 21)

1. sīsīpak
2. maskwak
3. sēhkēpayīsak
4. tēhtapiwina
5. wāpikwaniya
6. askihkwak
7. ospwākanak
8. kinēpikwak
9. iskwēwak

Spelling 3.2 (page 22)

1. sīsīpis
2. nīpin
3. tēpakohp
4. ayinānēwosāp
5. kinosēw
6. nihtiy
7. api
8. nakī
9. pasikō
10. itwē
11. niskīsik
12. kihtawakay
13. ocihciy
14. sēmāk
15. nimis
16. masinahikē
17. mitātaht
18. ayamihcikē
19. sīkaho
20. yīkowan

Exercise 3.1 (page 23)

1. askihk
2. minihkwācikan
3. anohc
4. oyākan
5. maskwa
6. pēyak
7. masinahikan
8. tēhtapiwin

Language Lab Session 4

Spelling 4.1 (page 32)

1. atim
2. tahkohc
3. sīpā
4. wayawītimihk
5. ispimihk
6. sīsīp
7. tāpwē
8. capisīs
9. anohc

Language Lab Session 5

Exercise 5.1 (page 36)

1. nāpēwak
2. astotin
3. Bill
4. oyākana
5. tēhtapiwina
6. piyēsīs
7. iskwēsisak
8. maskisin
9. nēhiyawak
10. masinahikana

Exercise 5.2 (page 37)

1. tānitē
2. tānēhki
3. kīkwāy

Exercise 5.3 (page 39)

1. awa
2. ōki
3. nēki
4. ōma
5. anima
6. nēhi
7. anihi
8. anihi
9. nēhi
10. ana

Spelling 5.1 (page 40)

1. tānēhki
2. kīspin
3. nāpēsis
4. piyēsīs
5. tānitē
6. tēpakohp
7. tāna
8. nakī
9. tāniwēhkāk
10. tāniwēhā
11. awāsis
12. iskwēsis
13. iskwāhtēm
14. tānisi
15. minōs
16. anohc
17. nāha
18. tāniwā
19. ospwākan
20. astotina

Spelling 5.2 (page 41)

1. api	5. itwē	9. mīciso
2. kīwē	6. pasikō	10. masinahikē
3. nakī	7. nipā	11. nīpawi
4. sīkaho	8. kwēskī	12. minihkwē

Language Lab Session 6

Spelling 6.1 (page 47)

1. nipāhpinān	11. masinahikēw
2. nēhiyawēw	12. mīcisowak
3. kimīcison	13. ninēhiyawān
4. kinipānāwāw	14. nitatoskānān
5. nipāwak	15. pāhpiw
6. kimasinahikān	16. nēhiyawēwak
7. nimīcisonān	17. pimohtēwak
8. mostohtēw	18. kimīcisonāwāw
9. kinēhiyawānaw	19. nimostohtānān
10. kipāhpinaw	20. atoskēw

Spelling 6.2 (page 48)

1. atāmihk	8. anohc	15. masinahikan
2. namōya	9. nāpēw	16. nimasinahikān.
3. pāhpiw.	10. nikotwāsik	17. sōniyāw
4. atoskēw.	11. iskwēsis	18. sīpiy
5. niyanān	12. mōswa	19. wāhyaw
6. tēpakohp	13. minōs	20. apisīs
7. tāniwē.	14. niyānan	21. tāpwē.

Language Lab Session 7

Spelling 7.1 (page 54)

1. yōtin
2. sīkipēstāw
3. pīwan
4. pahkipēstāw
5. ayamihēwi-kīsikāw
6. kisināw
7. wāsēskwan
8. yīkwaskwan
9. nēwo-kīsikāw
10. yīkowan
11. tahkāyāw
12. sōhkiyowēw

Spelling 7.2 (page 55)

1. kimiwan
2. nīso-kīsikāw
3. aywēstin
4. papēskwatāstan
5. kāmwātan
6. nisto-kīsikāw
7. wāsēskwan
8. sīkipēstāw
9. pīwan
10. niyānano-kīsikāw
11. mispon
12. kaskanawipēstāw
13. yīkwaskwan
14. nikotwāso-kīsikāw
15. tahkāyāw
16. kimiwasin
17. ayamihēwi-kīsikāw
18. pēyako-kīsikāw
19. yōtin
20. yīkowan

Exercise 7.1 (page 57)

Column B

a. 6
b. 10
c. 5
d. 1
e. 9
f. 2
g. 4
h. 3
i. 7
j. 8

Spelling 7.3 (page 58)

1. nīpin
2. pipon
3. sīkwan
4. piponohk
5. miyoskamiki
6. wāsēskwan
7. takwākohk
8. kisināw
9. takwākin
10. nīpinohk
11. miyoskamin
12. pipohki
13. sīkwanohk
14. nīpihki

Language Lab Session 9

Exercise 9.1 (page 69)

1. (1s) ē-pāhpiyān
2. (2s) ē-mīcisoyan
3. (2s) ē-nipāyan
4. (2s) ē-waniskāyan
5. (2s) ē-pāhpiyan
6. (3s) ē-apit
7. (3s) ē-ayamihcikēt
8. (3s) ē-masinahikēt
9. (3s) ē-kīwēt
10. (3's) ē-apiyit
11. (3's) ē-ayamihcikēyit
12. (3's) ē-masinahikēyit
13. (3's) ē-kīwēyit
14. (1p) ē-sipwēhtēyāhk
15. (1p) ē-pimohtēyāhk
16. (1p) ē-pimipahtāyāhk
17. (1p) ē-sēsāwipahtāyāhk
18. (21) ē-sipwēhtēyahk
19. (21) ē-pimohtēyahk
20. (21) ē-pimipahtāyahk
21. (21) ē-sēsāwipahtāyahk
22. (2p) ē-paminawasoyēk
23. (2p) ē-kīsitēpoyēk
24. (2p) ē-pahkwēsikanihkēyēk
25. (2p) ē-nīmāyēk
26. (3p) ē-itohtēcik
27. (3p) ē-mētawēcik
28. (3p) ē-pāhpicik
29. (3p) ē-pwātisimocik
30. (3'p) ē-nakīyit
31. (3'p) ē-mētawēyit
32. (3'p) ē-kotawēyit

Language Lab Session 10

Drill 10.1 (page 72)

1. <u>isiyihkāso</u>**w**. — <u>isiyihkāso</u>**yiwa**
2. <u>miywēyiht</u>**am** — <u>miywēyiht</u>**amiyiwa**
3. <u>masinahikē</u>**w**/<u>ayamihcikē</u>**w** — <u>ayamihcikē</u>**yiwa**
4. <u>mīciso</u>**wak** — <u>mīciso</u>**yiwa**
5. <u>tāhcipo</u>**w** — <u>tāhcipo</u>**yiwa**

Exercise 10.1 (page 74)

1. āpihtā-kīsikāki
2. tipiskohk
3. tipiskāw
4. otākosiki
5. wāpahki
6. pōn-āpihtā-kīsikāki

Language Lab Session 11

Exercise 11.1 (page 78)
Column B

a.	7	e.	3	i.	6
b.	10	f.	2	j.	8
c.	1	g.	4	k.	12
d.	5	h.	9	l.	11

CREE 101

Language Lab Session 12

Exercise 12.1 (page 81)
Note: The Independent and Conjunct inflections are highlighted in bold font.

	Verb Stems	Independent Inflections	Conjunct Inflections
1s	nikamo	**ni**nikamo**n**	ē-nikamo**yān**
2s	nipā	**ki**nipā**n**	ē-nipā**yan**
3s	mīciso	mīciso**w**	ē-mīciso**t**
3's	ayamihcikē	ayamihcikē**yiwa**	ē-ayamihcikē**yit**
1p	minihkwē	**ni**minihkwā**nān**	ē-minihkwē**yāhk**
21	pāhpi	**ki**pāhpi**naw**	ē-pāhpi**yahk**
2p	kawisimo	**ki**kawisimo**nāwāw**	ē-kawisimo**yēk**
3p	itohtē	itohtē**wak**	ē-itohtē**cik**
3'p	api	api**yiwa**	ē-api**yit**

Language Lab Session 13

Exercise 13.1 (page 91)

1. Future Conditional: wāsēskwahki
   English Translation: if/when it is sunny
   Present Tense Independent: wāsēskwan
   English Translation: it is sunny

2. Future Conditional: yōtiki
   English Translation: if/when it is windy
   Present Tense Independent: yōtin
   English Translation: it is windy

3. Future Conditional: sōhkiyowēki
   English Translation: if/when it very windy
   Present Tense Independent: sōhkiyowēw
   English Translation: it is very windy

4. Future Conditional: kimiwahki
   English Translation: if/when it rains
   Present Tense Independent: kimiwan
   English Translation: it is raining

5. Future Conditional: sīkipēstāki
   English Translation: if/when it is pouring
   Present Tense Independent: sīkipēstāw
   English Translation: it is pouring rain

6. Future Conditional: pahkipēstāki
   English Translation: if/when raindrops fall
   Present Tense Independent: pahkipēstāw
   English Translation: raindrops are falling

7. Future Conditional: kaskanawipēstāki
   English Translation: if/when it drizzles
   Present Tense Independent: kaskanawipēstāw
   English Translation: it is drizzling

8. Future Conditional: yīkwaskwahki
   English Translation: if/when it is cloudy
   Present Tense Independent: yīkwaskwan
   English Translation: it is cloudy

9. Future Conditional: yīkowahki
   English Translation: if/when it is foggy
   Present Tense Independent: yīkowan
   English Translation: it is foggy

10. Future Conditional: pīwahki
    English Translation: if/when it drifts
    Present Tense Independent: pīwan
    English Translation: it is drifting

11. Future Conditional: mispoki
    English Translation: if/when it snows
    Present Tense Independent: mispon
    English Translation: it is snowing

12. Future Conditional: āhkwatiki
    English Translation: if/when it is freezing
    Present Tense Independent: āhkwatin
    English Translation: it is freezing

13. Future Conditional: kisināki
    English Translation: if/when it is very cold
    Present Tense Independent: kisināw
    English Translation: it is very cold

14. Future Conditional: tahkāyāki
    English Translation: if/when it is cold
    Present Tense Independent: tahkāyāw
    English Translation: it is cold

15. Future Conditional: kisāstēki
    English Translation: if/when it is hot (weather)
    Present Tense Independent: kisāstēw
    English Translation: it is hot (weather)

16. Future Conditional: kisitēki
    English Translation: if/when it is hot
    Present Tense Independent: kisitēw
    English Translation: it is hot

17. Future Conditional: kīsapwēyāki
    English Translation: if/when it is warm (weather)
    Present Tense Independent: kīsapwēyāw
    English Translation: it is warm (weather)

18. Future Conditional: tihkitēki
    English Translation: if/when it melts
    Present Tense Independent: tihkitēw
    English Translation: it melts

19. Future Conditional: saskahki
    English Translation: if/when it is breakup
    Present Tense Independent: saskan
    English Translation: it is spring breakup

20. Future Conditional: kimiwasiki
    English Translation: if/when it rains a bit
    Present Tense Independent: kimiwasin
    English Translation: it is raining a bit

Language Lab Session 15

Exercise 15.1 (page 105)

	Dictation	**Translation**
1.	kiskinwahamākēw	teacher
2.	nōhkom	my grandmother
3.	ostēsa	his/her older brother
4.	ē-kisināk	as it is very cold
5.	ē-sīkipēstāk	as it is pouring (rain)
6.	onāpēma	her husband
7.	kiwīkimākan	your spouse/your husband/ your wife
8.	niyānanosāp	fifteen
9.	nitōtēm	my friend
10.	kimis	your older sister

Exercise 15.2 (page 106)

1. nitēm
2. otēma
3. kimosōm
4. nitasikan
5. nināpēm
6. kitiskwēm
7. otastotin

Language Lab Session 16

Exercise 16.1 (page 108)

1. (kī-)postiskamwak
2. (kī-)postiskamwak
3. nikī-wāpahtēn
4. kika-natonē(nā)naw
5. kinisitohtēn

Exercise 16.2 (page 110)

1. nika-pimohtatān
2. ta-pimohtatāwak
3. kikī-kīsihtān
4. kī-kātāw
5. nika-āpacihtānān

Exercise 16.3 (page 111)

1. nikī-mīcin
2. kī-wanihtāwak
3. kitayān
4. kikī-wanihtān
5. nikī-ayamihtānān

Language Lab Session 17

Exercise 17.1 (page 112)

The verbs stems in this short text are:

1. waniskā
2. tahkāyāw
3. itohtē
4. mīciso
5. wayawī
6. tahkāyāw
7. wāsēskwan
8. wāpam
9. nikamo
10. wīcēw
11. papāmipahtā

Exercise 17.2 (page 113)

1. itohtē/wāpam
   itohtē
2. mīciso
   mīciso
3. wīcēw
   wīcēw
4. kiyokaw
   wīcēw
   itohtē

Exercise 17.3 (page 114)

1. ocīmānimiwāw
2. wayawītimihk
3. mēskanāhk
4. mītosihk
5. kisēyiniw
6. misiwē

Language Lab Session 20

Drill 20.4 (page 127)

1. āha, nikī-ayamihtān pēyak masinahikan.
2. āha, nikī-miskēn astotin.
3. āha, ninisitohtēn nēhiyawēwin.
4. āha, ninōhtē-mīcin askipwāwa.
5. āha, nikī-yōhtēnēn wāsēnikan.
6. āha, niwāpahtēn atāwēwikamik.
7. āha, nitayān oyākan.

Exercise 20.1 (page 129)

1. masinahikan
2. oskinīkiskwēw
3. sākahikan
4. nikāwīnān
5. acimosis

About the Author

Jean Okimāsis was born Jean Lillian Littlechief to parents Dawson and Lillian (née Still) of White Bear First Nation in southeastern Saskatchewan. Her maternal grandparents were Joseph and Caroline (née Thomas) Still and her paternal grandparents were John and Annie (née Kakakaway) Littlechief. It is her small *kohkom*, Annie, who appears on the cover of the White Bear Conversational Cree CD and booklet along

with Jean (center) and her three cousins, Francis (standing next to Jean), Florence (far right), and Bernice (baby).

Jean received her elementary education on-reserve before completing high school at the Lebret Residential School. Jean holds a B.A. and LL.D. from the University of Regina.

During her university studies, Jean rediscovered a pride in her first language, Cree, and joined the late Dr. Ahab Spence in the fledgling Languages program at the Saskatchewan Indian Federated College (SIFC, which is now First Nations University of Canada) in 1982. Her own work, and collaboration with her student Solomon Ratt, quickly led to the publication of *Cree: Language of the Plains*, a language instructional set including textbook, workbook, and audio tapes, available from SIFC in many editions and printings through the 1980s and 1990s. These materials were eventually republished in 1999 by the Canadian Plains Research Center, with a major revision of the textbook completed in 2004. Jean's books and CDs are currently used in Cree language programs throughout western Canada.

At SIFC, Jean was a driving force behind the establishment of the Department of Indian Languages, Literatures, and Linguistics, for which she served as the first department head (1985–1988) and for a second term before her retirement from teaching (in 2002). She also contributed greatly to the creation of the first and only full degree programs in First Nations languages —Cree and Saulteaux (Ojibway)—in Canada. In spring 2005, Jean received an honorary Doctorate of Literature from the University of Regina.

Other accomplishments include her work on two First Nations language curricula (for Sask Learning and the Western Canadian Protocol), her constant participation in the Saskatchewan Cree Language Retention Committee, and numerous contributions to Cree language literacy through instruction, editing, and translation. In addition, Jean has made important contributions to the Algonquian Linguistic Atlas (www.atlas-ling.ca) and the ongoing research project "21st Century Tools for Indigenous Languages" (altlab.ualberta.ca/itwewina), partnering with the Universities of Alberta and Tromsø in Norway. Jean continues to work to transcribe recordings of the Elders.